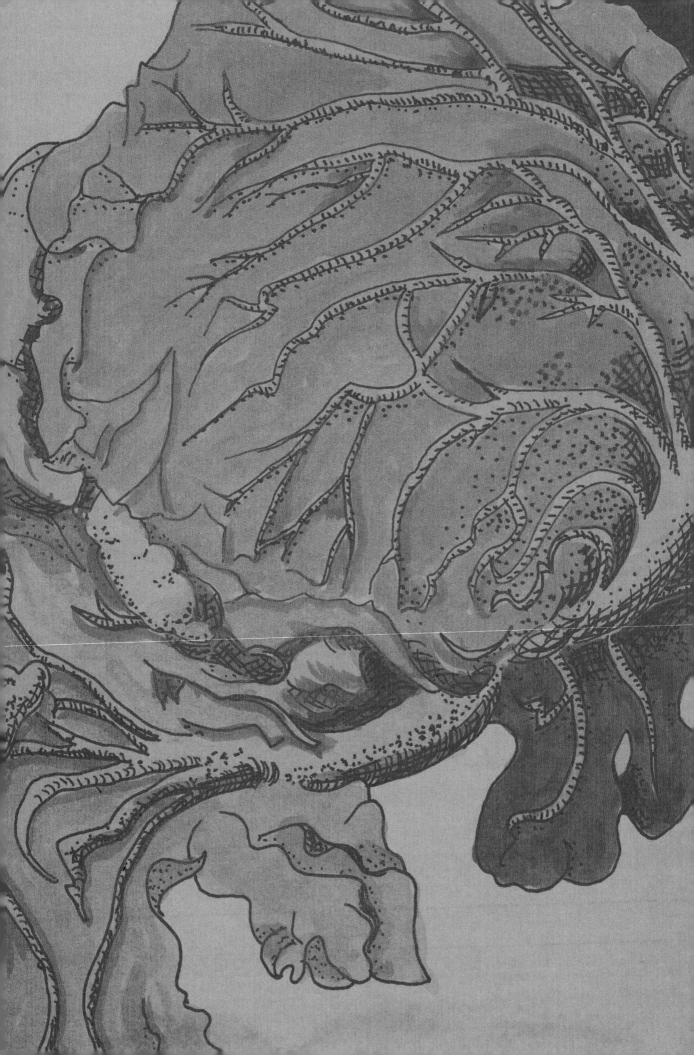

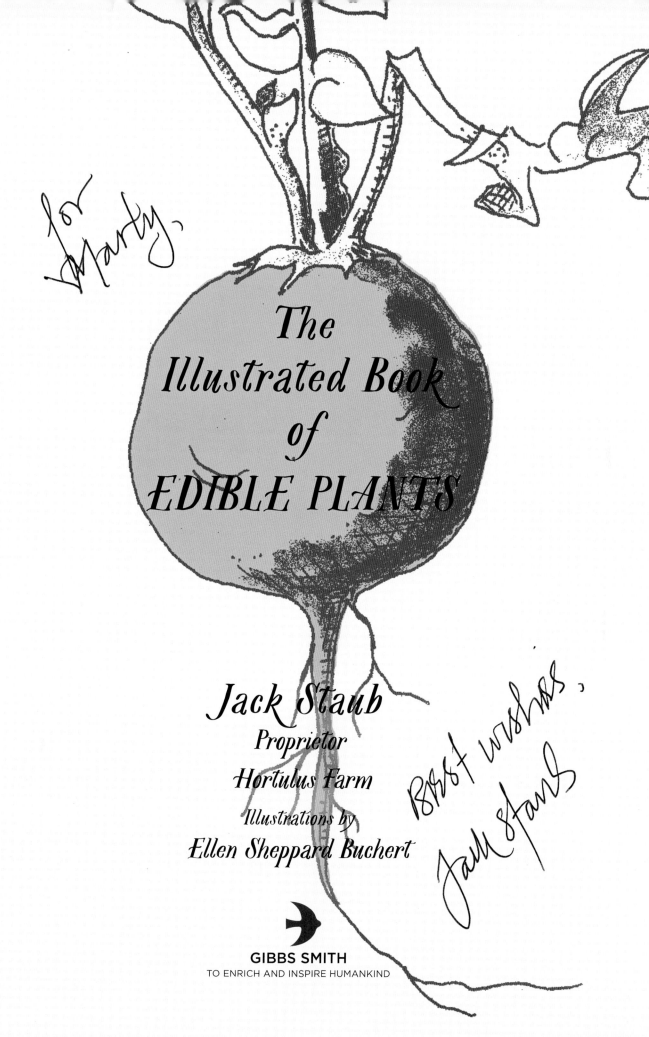

The
Illustrated Book
of
EDIBLE PLANTS

Jack Staub

Proprietor

Hortulus Farm

Illustrations by

Ellen Sheppard Buchert

GIBBS SMITH

TO ENRICH AND INSPIRE HUMANKIND

For Marty,

Best wishes,

Jack Staub

2

Contents

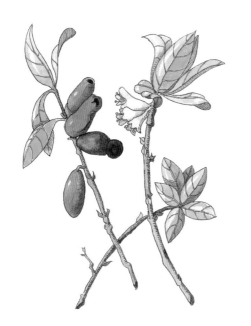

Preface

Growing much of what we eat has been one of the greatest joys of living at Hortulus Farm, and my passion for searching out unusual and interesting varieties of our common food plants remains unabated; so it is with great pleasure that I offer up to you eighty-five of the most winning edible plants on the planet.

The world truly is our horticultural oyster, with exciting new cultivars and even entirely unfamiliar species, like the goji and the honeyberry, coming to us from every corner of the globe. As well, in this tome, I urge you towards the cultivation of some of our lesser known edible plants, like anise, chervil, the persimmon, and the lingonberry, any of which will not only provide you with new culinary avenues to explore but plenty of visual delight in your garden. And then there are the fascinating histories, antique employments, myths and lore, however occasionally misguided, surrounding even our most familiar fruits, herbs, and vegetables.

Have I personally grown every plant, shrub, and tree in this book? No, and for fairly obvious cultural and climatic reasons, most particularly some of the finicky fruit trees that require a daunting regime of spraying, pruning, and fruit-thinning. That said, I have been vigilant in both research and visitation of neighboring farmers and orchardists, and the varietal information and cultural advice I impart to you here you may rely on.

My sincere hope is that you will find these plant portraits as enjoyable to browse as they are informative and that you will be inspired to culture some of these wonderful edible plants in your own garden. And if you're ever in our neighborhood, please do come see what we're growing on the farm!

Jack Staub
Hortulus Farm
www.hortulusfarm.com

Anise

Pimpinella anisum

*"For the dropsie, fill an old cock with Polipody and Aniseeds and
seethe him well, and drink the broth."*
–William Langham, *The Garden of Health*, 1633

*A*nise, also known as anise seed, pimpinel, and sweet cumin, is a member of the parsley family and, like many *umbellifers*, is thought to be anciently native to Egypt, Greece, and parts of the southern Mediterranean. According to excavated texts, anise has been cultivated in Egypt since at least 2000 B.C., the flavorful "seeds" having been employed as a diuretic, a digestive aid, and to relieve toothache. Anise is mentioned in the seventeenth-century-B.C. works of Hammurabi, the sixth king of Babylon and author of the *Code of Hammurabi*, one of the first legal treatises in recorded history, and it is also known that Charlemagne adored this fragrant herb and planted it extensively in his gardens at Aquisgrana between A.D. 800 and 814. Anise was known to British herbalists by the fourteenth century A.D. and, according to Mrs. Grieve, was being cultivated in Great Britain by the mid-sixteenth century, when it was also introduced into South America by the Spanish conquistadors. The *Pimpinella* in anise's botanical name derives from the Latin *dipinella*, or "twice pinnate," in reference to its leaf form, and because of its pungent, licorice sweetness, anise saw broad medicinal application across all cultures it touched, but particularly for respiratory and digestive ailments.

Hippocrates, father of modern medicine, recommended anise for respiratory issues in the fourth century B.C., and the Greek botanist Dioscorides wrote in the first century A.D. that anise "warms, dries, and dissolves" everything from an aching stomach and a sluggish digestion to excessive "winde" and a stinking breath. John Gerard recommended it in his *Herball* of 1636 for "the yeoxing or hicket [hiccup]" as well as "strengthening the coitus," and in 1763 Christopher Sauer maintained that it "removes chill from the chest" and "staves off coughing fits." The breath-sweetening employment was also lauded by the British apothecary William Turner, who reported in 1551 that "anyse maketh the breth sweter and swageth payne."

Interestingly, unlike many early herbal claims, most of those attached to anise are surprisingly smack on the money. We know now that anise seeds contain healthy doses of vitamin B, calcium, iron, magnesium, and potassium, as well as athenols, which aid in digestion, calm intestinal spasms, and reduce gas. A tisane made of anise has also proven effective in calming both coughs and chronic asthma, and, of course, anise is the main flavoring ingredient in those potent nectars anisette, pastis, and absinthe, the latter of which will pretty much calm anything into submission.

Anise is also a very pretty plant, with bright green coriander-like foliage and lovely, diminutive white-and-yellow flowers held in feathery umbels, the whole of it growing to about 18 inches.

Anise

Anise seeds are actually the fruit of the anise plant; when dried, they are transformed into those familiar gray/brown, longitudinally ribbed seeds habitually positioned as a digestif by the cash register in your favorite Indian restaurant. Anise is an annual herb and needs a longish, hot, dry season to seed successfully, so, in cooler climes, it is advisable to start seeds in pots indoors in March and set them out when the soil is well warmed up. Otherwise, sow seed in situ in dry, light soil and a sunny spot early in April, thinning the plants to about a foot apart. When threshed out, anise seeds are easily dried in trays and jarred for future use. In ancient Rome, wedding celebrations customarily ended with an anise-scented Mustacae cake to aid digestion (and, one assumes, "strengthen the coitus"), so why not create your own festivity by mixing a handful of anise seeds into your favorite pound cake recipe?

Apple

Malus domestica

The apple tree was so anciently regarded that in British lore,
Avalon, where King Arthur was taken to die, translates to
"Isle of Apples," and the Greek Elysium, where the worthy were
destined to spend their afterlives, to "Apple Land."

As we all know from that familiar Garden of Eden scenario, the apple is many millennia old, apple seeds having been found in Stone Age settlements in Switzerland dating to 8000 B.C. The tart wild crab apple *(Pyrus malus)*, native to the Caucasus and Turkey, is thought to be the ancient ancestor of the lot, and the first trees to produce our familiar sweet apple are believed to have grown near the modern city of Almaty, Kazakhstan. The cultivated apple, *Malus domestica*, has most probably been under global culture since the dawn of nearly any civilization you can name, Alexander the Great having been known to have imported dwarf apple types into Greece from Asia Minor in 300 B.C.

Along with their cousin the pear, apples are known botanically as "pomes," from the Latin *pomum*, or "orchard fruit," sharing the characteristics of a paper-like central core, crisp flesh around the core, and a thin outer skin. Interestingly, the apple has stood for both immortality – as in the precious apples doled out to the gods by the Nordic goddess Iduna to keep them forever young – and exactly the opposite, for the earthly cycle of birth, death, and rebirth. Pomona, the ancient Roman goddess of fertility and fruition, represented the apple's antique association with the great yearly cycle, this mandala-like imagery stemming from the apple's ostensible resemblance to the sun: born each day in pink apple-blossom clouds, ripening from yellow to red as it crosses the sky, ultimately to "drop" as if from a tree into the west.

Apples were first delivered to North America with Columbus in 1493, and records from the Massachusetts Bay Company indicate that apples were being grown in New England as early as 1630. Surely our most venerated American apple grower is the folk hero John Chapman of Leominster, Massachusetts, better known as "Johnny Appleseed." Living off the land during the first half of the nineteenth century, Johnny Appleseed founded countless orchards throughout Pennsylvania, Ohio, Michigan, Indiana, and Illinois. Today, in part thanks to John Chapman, there are more than 7,000 varieties of apples grown in the U.S., although a scant 20 varieties comprise more than 90 percent of our commercial apple industry. Some of the most popular are Cortland, Granny Smith, Red Delicious, Empire, Fuji, Gala, McIntosh, and Winesap; but why not search out some of the lesser known historical favorites like Ashmead's Kernel, Celestia, Esopus Spitzenberg, or Newtown Pippin, the latter two being preferred by Thomas Jefferson and George Washington, respectively.

Apples can be tricky in terms of procreation, as a seed from a chosen variety cannot be trusted to replicate its parent. Therefore, apple trees are generally created by grafting "scions," or shoots, which will grow true to species, onto accommodating rootstock. As well, all apple trees need cross-pollination to fruit successfully, so it will be necessary to companion plant with another type that blossoms at the same time to insure optimal yield. That said, apples are generally hardy and uncomplaining creatures, although they will grow best where winter temperatures hover near freezing for at least two months of the year, and one should take care to prune young trees during their formative years so that their branches are equally distributed. An apple tree will begin to bear fruit 6 to 8 years from planting but is then capable of producing fruit for up to an astonishing 100 years, which is a lot of applesauce. And that would be the perfect thing to do with any of your homegrown beauties!

Apple 'Celestia'

Apricot

Prunus armeniaca

In ancient Persia, the apricot was reverentially referred to as "the egg of the sun," and in the Near East, where the apricot flourishes, it is respectfully called "the moon of the faithful."

Northeastern China has been identified as this sunny, sweet-fleshed fruit's birthplace, most placing the date at about 1000 B.C. A *Prunus* member of the greater rose family, the apricot subsequently spread throughout Asia, ultimately wending its way into Armenia (thus *armeniaca*) by about 300 B.C. Apricots, however, appear to be a far-flung and generally unsociable family, as every region of every country in which the apricot thrives seems to have its own signature cultivar and little selection seems to have taken place anywhere within the apricot genus until the nineteenth century.

The word *apricock* first appeared in English print in 1551, deriving from the Latin *praecoquus,* also the root for *precocious* and, in this case, meaning "early ripening." Symbolically, the apricot, along with the peach and other stone fruits, was an ancient icon of female genitalia; in medieval France, for instance, the word *abricot* was a popular slang term for "vulva."

It was Franciscan missionaries who introduced the apricot to North America, and it was in the area south of San Francisco in 1792 that the first major U.S. production of apricots was recorded. Here, however, we come up against a somewhat cheerless truth: 95 percent of U.S.-grown apricots still come from California. To lunge straight to the heart of it, the apricot is a fruit plant with a tiresome propensity for swooning if the temperatures and climatic conditions are not wholly agreeable. For instance, apricots are keen on lots of moisture but not soggy feet, seem to prefer a cool, foggy summer and a damp, warm one equally, and can be broadly subject to loss of bloom or fruit by spring frost, while at the same moment requiring an adequately cold winter dormancy. "Difficult," as one would refer to a testy relative, I think about sums it up.

Apricot 'Blenheim'

10

Apricot 'Rival'

Medicinally, apricot seeds were used to treat tumors in an astonishingly early A.D. 502, and in Great Britain apricot oil was used as an erstwhile cure for tumors and ulcers throughout the seventeenth century. Interestingly, the wildly controversial drug Laetrile, ultimately disproved as a viable cancer therapy, was originally derived from an extract of apricot seeds. Modern medicine, however, does confirm that apricots are an excellent source of beta-carotene (one apricot will provide you with 10 percent of your daily recommended amount), vitamin C, iron, potassium, and fiber.

Apricots are truly lovely trees: small to medium-sized with a dense, spreading canopy, glossy reddish-brown bark, pretty heart-shaped leaves, and positive flurries of pretty white-to-pink *Prunus* blossoms. Another positive is that most U.S.-grown culti-vars are self-fruitful, so you only need to plant one. There are literally scores of apricot varieties, so if I haven't managed to dissuade you from attempting cultivation, it would pay to visit your local nursery and have them advise you about the likeliest prospects for your zone and climate. Although it can take 4 years for a young tree to begin fruiting, once established, a single tree can bear as much as 45 pounds of apricots a year for 20 years or more. Culturally, despite their need for regular waterings, try to keep in mind the finicky apricot's aversion to wet feet. Also, for optimal fruit size and harvest, you may want to thin your fruits to every 2 to 4 inches per branch. Our Viennese friends have historically plied us with mouthwatering apricot dumplings in season, wrapped in phyllo dough parcels and drenched in butter with a sprinkling of sugar, so here let me recommend that sumptuous recipe to you. Try to make two your limit.

Artichoke

Cynara scolymus

In 1948 in Castroville, California, "artichoke capital of the world," Norma Jean Baker (soon to be known as Marilyn Monroe) got her first leg up in life when she was elected the very first Artichoke Festival Queen.

The artichoke is the edible flower bud of a large, thistle-like plant of the sunflower family native to the Mediterranean and Near East, its common name coming to us from the Arabic *al kharshuf*. The Moroccan invaders brought the artichoke to Spain in the ninth or tenth century, whence it became *alcahofa*, the Italians subsequently turning it to *carciofa*. The Romans were fond of artichokes imported from Carthage and Cordova for their banquets, and thought the plants' spines looked like the teeth of Cynara, the dog of mythological tales; thus this cultivar's Latin sobriquet *Cynara scolymus*. In the first century A.D., the Roman naturalist Pliny noted, not with great pleasure, that in his time the artichoke was held in higher esteem than any other potherb in Rome, further commenting that even donkeys were smart enough to refuse to eat them.

Elizabethan folklore held that the artichoke, introduced into England in 1548, was created when an ill-tempered beauty angered the gods and was transformed by them into a prickly thistle, a form more suited to her personality. At the turn of the nineteenth century, the German poet Goethe was, like Pliny, appalled by the continental taste for artichokes, exclaiming incredulously in his *Travels Through Italy,* "The peasants eat thistles!" However, in Scotland around the same time, artichokes were so highly valued that it was thought only prosperous men should have the right to grow them and that it would be impertinent for a lesser man to even attempt such a folly.

Artichoke 'Opera'

Artichoke 'Gigante'

Artichoke 'Imperial'

Artichoke Hearts 'Opera'

Like many antique vegetables, artichokes were prescribed by ancient physicians for all kinds of physical ailments, from jaundice and coughs to the faltering libidos of men, the French herbalists Estienne and Liebault coyly suggesting in the sixteenth century that a diet rich in artichoke extracts could cure "weakness of the generative parts." The juice, when pressed from the plant before it blossomed, was also used as a popular hair restorative. We know now that artichokes are packed with phytonutrients and are highly efficacious in protecting against cancers, heart disease, liver dysfunction, high cholesterol, and diabetes. In fact, in terms of antioxidancy, in 2004 the USDA rated the artichoke seventh in the pantheon of edible plants.

If I had to pick one major piece of architecture to anchor a vegetable bed, an artichoke would be it. The most refined of thistles, these large, neatly carved, almost prehistoric-looking buds grow to magnificent proportions on sturdy 4- to 5-foot stems amid beautifully architectural, deeply cut, silver-green leaves that arch fountain-like from the crown. The Italians have made selections of both purple and green artichokes since the fifteenth century, the purple varieties, historically, thought to be more tender than the green types. Our most common artichokes are of the round, green "globe" variety, the most popular cultivars being 'Green Globe' and 'Imperial Star.' The Italian 'Violetto' types, like 'Opera', are more elongated in shape and prettily tinged with purple. When grown as perennials, artichokes have a life span of about five years and are propagated in winter or spring from root divisions. In Pennsylvania, where they are not hardy, I pot up my plants at the end of the season and overwinter them in the greenhouses. To culture annually, start seeds a good three months before your frost date, vernalize the plants for two weeks when temperatures hover in the 40s, then set out after danger of frost.

Culinarily, is there a yummier or healthier lunch than a cold, steamed artichoke with a bit of tarragon mayonnaise of a summer's day?

Female Asparagus in seed

Asparagus

Asparagus officinalis

*In the last century B.C., the Roman Emperor Caesar Augustus,
intent on mustering his troops at a more rapid pace,
coined the phrase velocius quam asparagi conquantur, translating
to "faster than you can cook asparagus."*

Asparagus, originally native to the eastern Mediterranean and Asia Minor, is a sufficiently ancient food plant to have been pictured, at least as a wild specimen, on an Egyptian frieze dating to 3000 B.C., and has been under human cultivation for at least 2,000 years. *Asparagus* comes to us from the Greek *asparagi,* meaning "sprout" or "shoot," and Julius Caesar was known to have enjoyed them anointed with melted butter. His heir, Caesar Augustus, was so enamored of this flavorsome edible that he initiated an entire "Asparagus Fleet" for the sole purpose of shipping the best specimens back to Rome with optimal speed while at the same time employing the Empire's fleetest athletes to transport fresh spears into the Alps, where they could be frozen for out-of-season enjoyment. Apicius, arguably the world's first cookbook author, included a recipe for preparing asparagus in the *De re coquinaria* of the third century A.D.; then, oddly, asparagus seems to have gone underground during the Middle Ages, only to make a dramatic comeback on the culinary scene in the sixteenth century. The spears, poetically noted to be "the size of a swan's feather," gained such fashionable status in France and England that Louis XIV himself proclaimed them "the food of kings" and they were deemed fit for the tables of the nobility alone. In the eighteenth century, asparagus gained quite a following as a purported aphrodisiac, the "love tips" (*"points d'amour"*) having been famously served as a delicacy to Madame de Pompadour at the court of Louis XV.

As it transpires, asparagus is an excellent source of vitamin B6, dietary fiber, calcium, and zinc, and a good source of protein, beta-carotene, vitamins C, E, and K, as well as folic acid, iron, phosphorus, potassium, copper, and manganese. All of these factors combine to make asparagus powerfully antioxidant as well as anti-inflammatory and an excellent diuretic in the promotion of kidney health.

Asparagus is available in both purple and green varieties, the purple types being the progeny of the Italian heirloom 'Violetto d' Albenga'. White asparagus are simply the result of blanching green spears as they grow by hilling up the earth around the crowns. Thanks mainly to plant breeders at New Jersey's Rutgers University, today's improved and all-male strains of asparagus, like 'Jersey Giant', 'Jersey Supreme', and 'Jersey Knight', are far easier to plant than the antique cultivars like the female 'Martha Washington' and produce almost twice as much in the bargain.

Therefore, in early spring, prepare a weed-free, well-fertilized bed large enough to accommodate two dozen male asparagus crowns spaced 12 to 18 inches apart in two side-by-side trenches 6 to 12 inches deep. Situate each crown on a mound of compost enhanced with an organic fertilizer with some phosphorus content about 6 inches below the soil surface, allowing the roots to drape down around the mound. Cover the roots with garden soil right up to the crown, water well, and as shoots develop add more soil until the trench has been filled level with the soil surface. Keep your bed well mulched, well watered, and weed free, and don't pick *any* of the spears the first year, as the crowns get their energy from the ferny growth that develops as the tips mature into fronds. By the third year, a modest planting of two dozen male crowns will start yielding up to 20 pounds of edible spears per year for a very impressive fifteen to twenty years!

In terms of culinary employment, shall we harken back to Julius Caesar and that melted butter idea with just a squeeze of lemon?

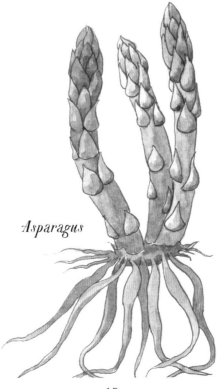

Asparagus

Basil

Ocimum basilicum

Chrysippus, the ancient Greek champion of stoic theory, reported as early as the third century B.C., that "ocimum exists only to drive men insane."

*I*t's interesting that a plant as benignly loveable as our common sweet basil *(Ocimum basilicum)* developed in such a swirl of historical controversy and opposing symbolism. Thought to have originated in India, at least in the form of holy basil *(Ocimum sanctum),* basil is also incredibly ancient to both Africa and Asia, although the compact bush basil *(Ocimum minimum)* is native to South America alone. Basil is thought to have entered Greece with the returning armies of Alexander the Great in about 350 B.C., ultimately reaching England and northern Europe in the early sixteenth century and the North American continent through the earliest Spanish explorers in the late sixteenth century.

The term *basil* seems to have two possible derivations: the first from the terrifying half-lizard, half-dragon *basilisk* of Greek mythology and the second from the Greek basilikon, meaning "royal" or "kingly," in reference to basil's regal scent and royal-purple flower wand. In India, holy basil (*tulasi*) is regarded as sacred, being associated with the goddess Tulasi, who, after being tricked by Vishnu into betraying her husband and then killing herself, was worshipped ever after for her faithfulness, tulasi ultimately becoming a Hindu symbol of love, purity, and protection.

In ancient Greece and Rome, however, it was bizarrely decided that basil would only grow well if you shrieked wild curses while sowing the seed, and in France you can still hear the phrase *semer le basilic,* which translates to "sowing the basil," meaning "to rant and rave." Basil also developed an equally bizarre reputation for spontaneously generating scorpions as per the seventeenth-century French botanist Joseph Pitton de Tournefort: "A certain Gentleman of Siena was wont to take the powder of the dry herb and snuff it up his nose; but in a short time he turned mad and died; and his head being opened by surgeons, there was found a nest of scorpions in his brain."

On a lighter, amatory note, in old Romania, if a girl presented her beau with a sprig of basil, they were officially engaged, and Italian suitors traditionally signaled their love by courting with a sprig of basil tucked behind one ear; in many parts of Italy, basil still goes by the charming alter ego *bacia-nicola,* or "Kiss-Me-Nicholas."

In the end, what is one to think? The British herbalist Nicholas Culpeper had a very clear idea when, in 1653, he deemed basil ". . . the Herb which all Authors are together by the Ears about, and rail at one another like Lawyers."

What seems beyond contemporary debate, however, is that basil in any of its lovely scented forms is an easy-to-grow annual and a seasonal staple in the kitchen. Aside from those previously mentioned, some other varieties that may be of interest are the classic big-leaved 'Genovese' type; the spicy 'Thai' variety with a hint of cinnamon; the tiny-leaved 'Globe', perfect for pot culture; the sprightly 'Lemon' or 'Lime' types, scented with a hint of citrus; and the purple and ruffled varieties like 'Red Rubin', 'Opal', or 'Purple Ruffles', which add a becoming flash of color to the garden. The latest basil rage is 'Pesto Perpetuo' (*Ocimum* x *citriodorum*), a recently developed hybrid praised for its unique variegated, non-flowering, columnar habit, although it's only available for purchase as a plant.

In any case, no matter what variety of basil you choose, do sow some seeds or transplant a few plants into a nice, sunny position in the garden, keep the flower heads clipped on most types, hoard a bit of fresh mozzarella, and wait patiently for the first garden tomato and the culinarily *ne plus ultra* of a classic Caprese salad.

Bay Laurel

Laurus nobilis

In a notable herbal leap of faith, the thirteenth-century Arab physician Ibn al-Baitar believed that sporting a bay leaf behind one's ear could prevent inebriation.

The true culinary bay laurel *(Laurus nobilis)*, also known as sweet bay, is antiquely native to the Mediterranean, India, and Africa alone, although its cousin in the greater magnolia family, the California bay *(Umbellularia californica)*, also known as Oregon myrtle and pepperwood, is a close ringer but of a stronger savor. The ancient Greeks considered the *Laurus nobilis* both sacred and protective and associated it with Apollo, who fashioned himself a crown of laurel to celebrate the slaying of Python, the tempestuous she-dragon of the underworld, upon whose former lair he built his Delphic temple and then roofed it with bay leaves to protect it from lightning. Similar celebratory wreaths were soon bestowed upon the winning athletes of the Pythian games at Delphi, ultimately graced the locks of the first Olympians, and were awarded to the greatest early poets – thus "poet laureate" – with our educationally esteemed baccalaureate, translating to "laurel berry."

Additionally, the Pythia, the anciently revered Apollonian Oracle of Delphi, is known to have chewed bay leaves to intensify her oracular hallucinations, famously delivered in an ecstatic trance and partially induced by what contemporary historians now believe were ethylene vapors rising from fissures in the ground around her. Greek mythology also gives to this savory herb its Greek name Daphne, in reference to the beautiful nymph daughter of the river god Peneios and earth goddess Ge, whom they transformed into a bay laurel in order that she might escape the prurient advances of Apollo. From that moment on, the bay laurel was associated with purity, purification, and protection, with Nicholas Culpeper jumping onto the "protective" bandwagon in his *Complete Herbal* of 1653 and attributing all kinds of pharmacological feats to the bay laurel, including the berries being "very effectual against all poisons of venomous creatures" and the oil distilled from them helping with "palsies, convulsions, cramps, aches, trembling, and numbness of any part."

Contemporarily, because of the bay laurel's strong camphorous fragrance, it is most generally herbally employed as an aromatherapy oil in the treatment of such complaints as colds, flu, and muscle aches. It is, however, its famous culinary merits that remain truly commendable.

Additionally, *Laurus nobilis* is a handsome tree with signature thick, shiny, elliptical leaves, small pale-yellow flowers, and oval green berries, which will ultimately turn black in fall. That said, here I am forced to admit that the bay laurel is hardy only to USDA zones 8 through 10 and is a somewhat delicate creature, craving protection from frost (a good, thick mulching of its notably shallow root system) and wind (a sunny, sheltered location), and requiring rich, well-drained soil.

Bay Laurel

However, as many ancient households habitually displayed a "protective" potted bay beside the front door to ward off evil spirits, it is this employment I will recommend to the greatest number of you here. The bay laurel is a splendid candidate for pot culture and, loving a good spring pruning, may be kept to a manageable 6 to 8 feet tall as well as topiaried to suit your aesthetic whim. Just pot up in light, well-drained soil, keep in a cool, dry, brightly lit spot indoors in winter, and move outdoors to a partially shaded locale in summer.

Culinarily, what could be more entrancing than to harvest bay leaves off your very own tree (n.b.: leaves don't develop their full gusto until several weeks after picking and drying), tie them up with some fresh thyme and parsley, and add them to your favorite recipe in the flavorful guise of a classic bouquet garni. As Julia Child so aptly and frequently put it, "Bon appétit!"

Bean

Phaseolus vulgaris

*Pythagoras, the great Greek mathematician, held the decidedly
unscientific and highly unlikely belief that
human souls transmigrated into beans after death.*

*L*et us here clear up once and for all this idea of the "green" bean. Green beans *(Phaseolus vulgaris)* versus broad or fava beans (var. *Vicia faba*), which are the European variety, originated in the Americas alone and were only introduced into Europe by the Spanish in the sixteenth century. Green beans can actually be myriad colors, from burgundy through regulation green to brilliant yellow; they were called "green" as they were eaten green, i.e., when young with pod and all, to distinguish them from *Vicia faba*, which are only eaten dried or shelled. Additionally, green beans of any color can be either of the pole (vining and climbing) or bush (compact, low-growing) habit.

Historically, man has always had somewhat of a love-hate relationship with the bean. In ancient Rome, for instance, a pontifex of the official Roman religion was forbidden to eat or even utter the word *bean,* as funerals generally ended with a feast of beans and they were, therefore, considered inauspicious. In Egypt, priests considered them unclean. Whether this was at all related to the Pythagorian theory that that darling fava on your plate might by harboring the soul of your dear departed mama is unknown. On the American continent, Native Americans historically planted the "three sisters," – corn, squash, and beans – together, as the corn stalks provided nicely

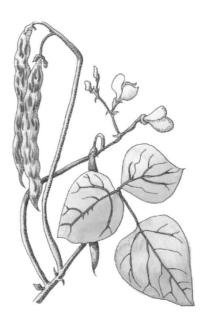

Bean 'Dragon Tongue'

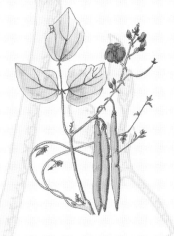

Runner Bean 'Painted Lady'

Runner Bean 'Golden Sunshine'

Chinese Long Bean 'Yard Long White Snake'

accommodating trellising for the trailing squash and beans.

There are countless excellent cultivars in both the pole and bush categories from which to choose, now selected and available from all corners of the globe, ranging from pencil-thin green filets to broad, flat Romano types to the non-Phaseolus varieties like the prettily blossomed, Central America-bred Runner types *(P. coccineus)* like 'Painted Lady' and the chartreuse-leaved 'Golden Sunshine' to the startling Chinese Long Beans (*Vigna unguiculata* subsp. *sesquipedalis*) like 'Red Noodle' and 'Yard Long White Snake', the *sesquipedalis* translating to foot and a half long, which gives you some idea of their unique allure (although it is interesting to note that beans came to China only in about A.D. 1200). Here I will pause to recommend a few types we grow annually on the farm, noting that every home gardener should grow beans, as legumes are the only food plants that will actually enrich rather than deplete your soil by reaffixing nitrogen there. In terms of pole beans, we always plant the round-podded varieties Fortex and the wax bean Monte Gusto, the Romano types Helda and Golden of Bacau, and certainly one of the Chinese Long Beans. In terms of bush types, we like the purple-and-gold-splotched Dragon Tongue, the purple Royal Burgundy Pod, and the thin filets Maxibel and Roc d'Or.

A true health powerhouse, 100 grams of beans will give you 20 percent of your daily dose of vitamin C and 13 percent of vitamin A along with a healthy swat of B vitamins, plenty of protein, fiber, and folic acid, plus a positive battery of minerals and phytonutrients, including carotenoids and flavonoids. All these amount to substantial benefits in helping to control glucose in diabetics and aiding in both digestive and heart health, increased metabolism, and an enhanced immune system. In terms of culture, beans cannot abide cold soil, so direct sow seeds when temperatures are well warmed up, the bush types spaced about 10 inches apart and the pole types around the circumference of an accommodating teepee. Additionally, because of their shallow root growth, beans require adequate watering, particularly in hot weather.

In my opinion, beans are optimally prepared when they are just picked, steamed briefly, drained and refreshed, then tossed with a knob of butter, a shake of salt and pepper, a sprinkle of lemon juice, and a handful of chopped fresh herb, like tarragon, basil, or mint.

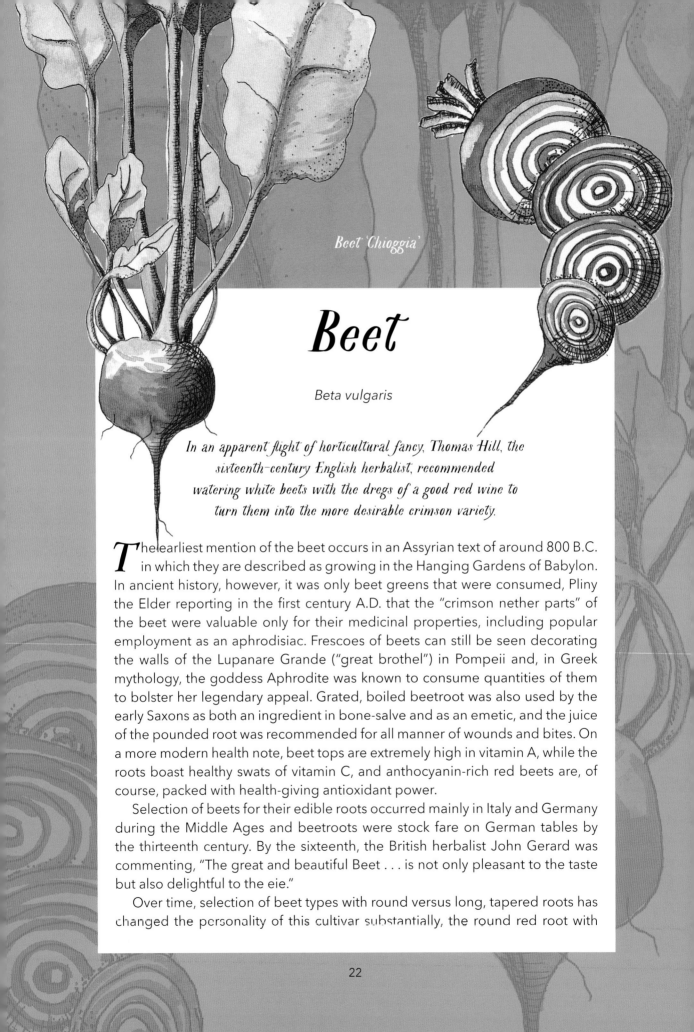

Beet 'Chioggia'

Beet

Beta vulgaris

*In an apparent flight of horticultural fancy, Thomas Hill, the
sixteenth-century English herbalist, recommended
watering white beets with the dregs of a good red wine to
turn them into the more desirable crimson variety.*

The earliest mention of the beet occurs in an Assyrian text of around 800 B.C. in which they are described as growing in the Hanging Gardens of Babylon. In ancient history, however, it was only beet greens that were consumed, Pliny the Elder reporting in the first century A.D. that the "crimson nether parts" of the beet were valuable only for their medicinal properties, including popular employment as an aphrodisiac. Frescoes of beets can still be seen decorating the walls of the Lupanare Grande ("great brothel") in Pompeii and, in Greek mythology, the goddess Aphrodite was known to consume quantities of them to bolster her legendary appeal. Grated, boiled beetroot was also used by the early Saxons as both an ingredient in bone-salve and as an emetic, and the juice of the pounded root was recommended for all manner of wounds and bites. On a more modern health note, beet tops are extremely high in vitamin A, while the roots boast healthy swats of vitamin C, and anthocyanin-rich red beets are, of course, packed with health-giving antioxidant power.

Selection of beets for their edible roots occurred mainly in Italy and Germany during the Middle Ages and beetroots were stock fare on German tables by the thirteenth century. By the sixteenth, the British herbalist John Gerard was commenting, "The great and beautiful Beet . . . is not only pleasant to the taste but also delightful to the eie."

Over time, selection of beet types with round versus long, tapered roots has changed the personality of this cultivar substantially, the round red root with

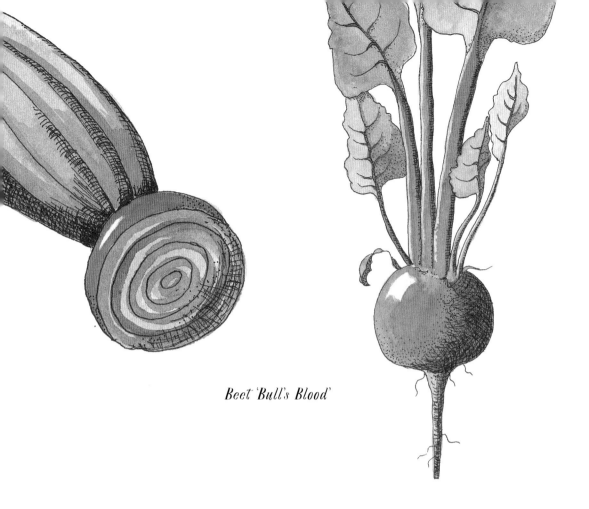

Beet 'Bull's Blood'

which we are familiar having been developed at Castelnaudary, in the Languedoc region of France, in the early nineteenth century. Modern table beets, however, may still come in a broad variety of colors, from black and red to purple, gold, and white, and in every silhouette from round or oval to cylindrical.

Some of the most popular regulation reds are 'Avenger', 'Gladiator', 'Red Ace', and 'Big Red'. However, why not head to one of the more exotic types like 'Bull's Blood', notable for its very tasty, deep purple, nearly black tops; 'Golden', a buttery yellow, mild-fleshed charmer; and 'Chioggia', an Italian heirloom introduced to American gardeners in the late 1840s and offering up a bit of pink-and-white bull's-eye op art when one cuts into it.

Beets are cool-season plants that grow best at temperatures between 60 and 65 degrees, the optimum soil temperature for seed germination being 55 to 75 degrees; so direct sow in early spring as soon as you can work the soil. Although some avow that beets will tolerate part shade, I'm of the experience that they require full sun and will not make good roots without it. As with all root crops, a well-turned soil is essential and a light, sandy loam ideal, permitting the longed-for rapid, uninterrupted growth of roots; in heavy or poorly drained soils, you might even consider preparing a raised bed for them. Space plants 2 to 4 inches apart, then thin them to 4 to 6 inches when plants are 2 to 3 inches tall. You can expect to harvest anywhere from 55 to 70 days after sowing, and you can clip the greens in just 30 to 45 days.

Whatever variety you choose to plant, consider employing them in a summery roasted beet and feta salad: wrap each beet in tin foil, bake at 400 degrees until easily pierce-able, cool, peel, slice, and toss with feta crumbles and a lively vinaigrette.

Blackberry

Rubus fruticosus

*In England, it was anciently held that passing beneath
an arch of brambles would cure everything from
rheumatism and boils to whooping cough and blackheads.*

Blackberries are so weedily invasive in so many parts of the globe, their native distribution ranging from the Arctic to the tropics and on every continent save Antarctica, that many would positively snort at the suggestion that one might choose to plant one. Botanists still cannot decide whether there was a single original blackberry that gave birth to the current baffling array of global relations, or, in fact, every sector of the globe gave birth to its own brood of favored offspring. They have been consumed since Neolithic times and were so generally employed as a thorny, marauder-dissuading hedgerow that John Gerard commented in his *Herball* of 1636, "the bramble groweth for the most part in every hedge and bush."

In Europe and Asia alone there are over 2,000 named varieties and 66 separate species. Then there is that gaggle of non-blackberries, known by various aliases like dewberry, loganberry, boysenberry, tayberry, youngberry, olallieberry, and marionberry, all mainly named by and for their developers yet virtually identical to their blackberry cousins save for their growing habit. To my mind, they are all variations on a dewberry *(Rubus pubescens)* theme, as rather than growing on erect caning bushes, these suspect siblings exhibit a crawly habit and are commonly grown on trellises. Blackberries have been known antiquely by many names, including "brambleberry" and "brumblekite," derived from the Old English *brymbyl*, for "prickly."

Thornless Blackberry 'Oregon Cutleaf'

John Gerard lauds them as a valuable astringent, serving to "heal the eies that hang out," while also noting that "the leaves of the bramble boiled in water with honey, alum, and a little white wine" would "fastneth the teeth." On a more modern medical note, blackberries are wonderfully rich in bioflavonoids and Vitamin C and have one of the highest antioxidant levels of all fruits, and their enviable tannin content can help reduce intestinal inflammation and alleviate hemorrhoids.

With their brambly, weedy reputation, it should be apparent that, once planted, you can fairly kick sand in a blackberry's face and it will respond by flourishing and fruiting without a wince. That said, some varieties will do better in your zone and climate than others, so it will pay to consult a local nursery for your best option. Some of the most popular modern thorn-bearing varieties are 'Darrow', 'Illini Hardy', 'Kiowa', 'Prime Jan', and 'Prime Jim', but why not head to a thornless variety for less painful picking? A few that top that list are 'Apache', 'Arapaho', 'Black Satin', 'Chester', 'Triple Crown', and 'Oregon Cutleaf'.

Blackberries are perennials that produce on one- and two-year-old "canes," the first-year canes (primocanes) growing without flowering, the second-year canes (floricanes) flowering, fruiting, and expiring within that season. Culturally, the best idea is to prune back the entire stand to 12 inches following harvest so that some primocane growth will occur before frost. Dewberry types are more prone to frost damage, so their cultural key is to remove the spent floricanes after fruiting, prune to the strongest 6 or 8 primocanes, coil them onto the ground, and mulch heavily. In spring, unearth the primocanes (now floricanes), and reattach them to your trellising.

In terms of employment, blackberry wines and cordials have provided man with an excellent pick-me-up across countless centuries and cultures, so why not give this ancient receipt a try? Crush a big pot of blackberries, adding one quart of boiling water for each gallon of fruit, allow to stand for a day, strain off the solids, add 2 pounds of sugar for every gallon of liquid, pour the result into a becoming vessel, and keep tightly corked. A year hence, let the games begin!

Blueberry

Vaccinium corymbosum

*Early Native Americans believed that the five-pointed star
at the blossom end of each blueberry signified that the
berries were a gift from the Great Spirit sent to relieve their
hunger during times of famine.*

Many botanists believe a blueberry antecedent could be the most ancient living thing on earth, stepping up to the cereal bowl at a whopping 13,000 years old. There are *Vaccinium* varieties native to virtually everywhere, including Europe, Scandinavia, the Far and Middle East, and both Americas. Therefore, the extended blueberry family includes countless permutations on a theme, every zone and climate having its own undomesticated variety as well as a number of modern cultivars selected and hybridized from the wild.

Also known historically as "bilberries," "whortleberries," and "hurtleberries," John Gerard described both a black and a red "wortle" in his *Herball* of 1636, noting that the black variety is "full of a pleasant and sweet juyce" which does "colour the mouth and lips of those that eat them." Both Virgil and Pliny lauded the virtues of their native *Vaccinium*, and blueberries have certainly figured in the native diet of the Americas since prehistory, the French explorer Samuel de Champlain noting in 1615 that the Indians of the Great Lakes region not only harvested but venerated the blueberry.

On an extremely healthy note, the flavonoids in blueberries give them the highest antioxidant capacity of any commonly consumed fruit; they're high in vitamins C and K as well as fiber; and contemporary studies have shown that they can not only help lower blood pressure but protect against both DNA damage and oxidative damage from LDL ("bad" cholesterol).

Blueberry 'Sunshine'

Blueberry 'Rubel'

To certainly oversimplify, there are three basic types of "true" blueberry, mainly grown on the American continent: Highbush *(Vaccinium corymbosum)*, Lowbush *(Vaccinium angustifolium)*, and Rabbiteye *(Vaccinium ashei)*. As their names would suggest, Highbush are erect shrubs and Lowbush are squat and crawly; Rabbiteye, named for their beady berries, are also erect shrubs. Equally simplistically, each of these three varieties is defined in part by its favored home: in eastern North America, Lowbush types are adapted from Canada down through Maine, Highbush types from New England down through the Carolinas, and Rabbiteyes from the Carolinas down to Florida. Then, to confound things further, two stellar hybrids have leapt upon the *Vaccinium* scene, the first being the 'Southern Highbush', a cross between a Northern Highbush, a Rabbiteye, and an Evergreen blueberry (V. *darrowii*), the second being the Half-High Highbush, a cross between a Northern Highbush and a Lowbush. As well, there are early, mid-season, and late-season varieties of each subset; so, in the end, it will pay to consult your local Cooperative Extension for the best choice for your needs. Some of the most popular in each category are the Highbush darlings 'Bluetta', 'Patriot', 'Jersey', 'Pioneer', and 'Legacy'; the Lowbush favorites 'Brunswick', 'Burgundy', and the dwarf 'Tophat'; the Rabbiteyes 'Bonita' and 'Climax'; the Southern Highbush varieties 'Rebel', 'Star', 'Sunshine Blue', and 'Windsor'; and the Half-High types 'Chippewa', 'Northblue', and 'Polaris'.

Blueberries, in general, will prefer a slightly acidic soil (pH 4.5 to 5.2), will benefit from a nice dressing of organic matter, and will not tolerate nitrate nitrogen-based fertilizers; so head in the direction of one of the ammonium sulfate-based brands used for azaleas and rhododendrons. As well, many wild blueberry farmers still employ the ancient Native American trick of burning a portion of their fields to the ground annually, a practice which serves to kill insects, control funguses and, most importantly, stimulate growth.

In terms of culinary employment, does anyone really need any advice? If so, John Gerard observed in his celebrated *Herball* that "the people of Cheshire do eat blacke Wortles in cream and milk, as in these South parts we eat Strawberries," which sounds like a lovely idea.

Borage

Borago officinalis

"Ego borago gaudia semper ago."
("I, borage, always bring joy.")

—Ancient Latin proverb

Native in some gauzy mist of time to the Aleppo region of Syria but now natural-ized as a garden escapee in much of Europe and North America, borage has long been prized for its herbal, culinary, and decorative virtues. Some believe *borage* derives from a corruption of the Latin *cor,* for "heart," and *ago,* "I bring," in reference to this plant's legendary deliverance of "joy" or "courage" to whomever might sup on or sip of it, for one historical fact seems to emerge eminently clearly: borage *(Borago officinalis)* seemed to make everyone happy – quite literally. In fact, it was Pliny the

28

Elder himself, in his *Naturalis Historia* of A.D. 77, who first lauded borage's ability to ". . . maketh a man merry and joyful," and Sir Francis Bacon, English statesman and father of both the modern essay and the Baconian method of scientific deduction, writes at the beginning of the seventeenth century that borage ". . . hath an excellent spirit to repress the fuliginous vapour of dusky melancholie." John Gerard, in his *Herball* of 1636, expounds on borage in this fashion: "Those of our time do use the flowers in sallads to exhilerate and make the mind glad . . . The leaves and floures of Borage put into wine make men and women glad and merry and drive away all sadnesse, dulnesse and melancholy, as Dioscorides and Pliny affirme. [Dioscorides and Pliny also maintained that borage was the famous nepenthe of Homer, which, when consumed in wine, induced blissful forgetfulness.] Syrup made of the floures of Borage comforteth the heart, purgeth melancholy and quieteth the phrenticke and lunaticke person." In the same century, John Parkinson commends borage ". . . to expel pensiveness and melanchollie," and John Evelyn, in his *Acetaria* of 1679, reports, ". . . the Sprigs in Wine . . . are of known Vertue to revive the Hypochrondriac and chear the hard student." Is everyone ready to order a case?

While modern medicine does not really substantiate this whole "joy," "revive," and "chear" thing, it does confirm that borage is not only a fantastic source of vitamins A and C but also contains healthy amounts of potassium and calcium, with the stems and leaves delivering admirable quantities of saline mucilage, and it is to these enviable saline qualities that the historic invigorating properties of borage are currently pinned. As well, in 1985, widespread cultivation of borage in North America was begun for the purpose of harvesting borage seed, the oil of which contains 20 to 23 percent Gamma-linolenic acid (GLA), almost twice as much as other sources. Research shows that GLA has huge potential in the treatment of the symptoms of rheumatoid arthritis.

Now consider borage's distinctive woolly, gray-green, languidly drooping form growing in a stout rosette to 2 or 3 feet and its gorgeous bright blue star-shaped blossoms with their signature black "beauty marks" (anthers, actually), and I believe we are on to something.

The flavor of borage is refreshingly cucumber-y, the leaves being excellent steamed or sautéed, the stems peeled and used like celery, and the fresh flowers showstopping in salads and, candied, on desserts. In medieval England, borage leaves were steeped in wine or cider with lemon and sugar to create a "cool tankard" and, one assumes, a little happiness on a sweltering summer's eve. Contemporary astrologer and herbalist Jonathan Pearl, however, recommends this "joy"-ful elixir to banish melancholy: loosely pack a blender with fresh borage leaves, pour in dry vermouth to cover, pulse into a green soup, let sit for 6 hours, strain, bottle, refrigerate, and sip as your mood dictates.

Broccoli

Brassica oleracea

Broccoli, as a member of the *Brassica* family, is so closely related to cauliflower, cabbage, and Brussels sprouts in genetic disposition that botanists have always had difficulty with their classification. All *Brassicas* share a common feature in that their four-petaled flowers bear a resemblance to a Greek cross, which is why they are frequently referred to as "crucifers," and the name *broccoli* comes from the Latin *bracchium,* meaning "strong arm" or "branch," broccoli having many strong "branches" or "arms" growing from the stout main stem.

An ancient Etruscan cultivar, broccoli is actually thought to have been introduced into culture by the Rasenna, who immigrated to Italy from what is now Turkey in the eighth century B.C. The ancient Rasenna proved to be active traders with the Greeks, Sicilians, Corsicans, and Sardinians, and so broccoli spread rapidly through the Greco-Roman empire, Pliny the Elder reporting that the inhabitants of Rome grew and enjoyed broccoli during the first century B.C., where the most common green-headed variety, 'Calabrese,' was first developed, Roman farmers glowingly referring to it as "the five green fingers of Jupiter." It was the Tuscan-born Catherine de' Medici who is believed to have introduced broccoli into France upon her

Purple Sprouting
Broccoli

Broccoli 'Romanesco'

marriage to Henry II in 1533. At the court of Elizabeth I, it was referred to as "brawcle," and in 1699, the English herbalist John Evelyn reports in his *Acetaria* that "the broccoli from Naples . . . are very delicate . . . [and] commended for being not so rank, but agreeable to most palates and of better nourishment." By 1775, Thomas Jefferson's cousin the controversial Virginia congressman John Randolph was describing it in *A Treatise on Gardening by a Citizen of Virginia,* advising erstwhile consumers that "the stems will eat like asparagus, and the heads like cauliflower."

However, despite this heartening description, broccoli was initially received in North America with what can only be described as stunning indifference, and right up to the 1920s, many Americans continued to disdain it as being a component of the peasant diet of Italian immigrants. In fact, it wasn't really until the mid-twentieth century that broccoli finally took hold in the United States, and in the past half century, due to broccoli's now famously vitamin-rich reputation, consumption has increased by a very healthy 940 percent. All broccolis are, in fact, jewels of nutrition, being uncommonly rich in vitamin A, potassium, iron, fiber, beta-carotene, and a host of anticarcinogens. There are many fine cultivars, ranging from the familiar brawny 'Calabrese' variety to the spiraling, apple-green whorls of broccoli 'Romanesco' to the to the thin, leafy, pleasantly bitter stalks of that broccoli cousin Broccoli Raab to the wonderfully tender shoots of the English-bred Sprouting Broccolis.

With the exception of the sprouting types, which may be planted in the fall in American zones 7 through 10 and harvested in the early spring, broccolis are cool-weather vegetables. Therefore, start the large-headed types indoors 4 weeks before your frost date, plant out after danger of frost 15 inches apart in fertile soil, and expect to start harvesting 75 to 100 days from transplant. Broccoli Raab may be direct seeded in the garden as soon as the soil can be worked about 2 inches apart, thinned to 4 to 6 inches, and harvested in about 40 to 60 days. In terms of culinary employment, for the ubiquitous 'Calabrese' types, my advice is to lightly peel the stem like you would an asparagus, cut the head in half, steam until tender but still bright green, and serve, one-half head per serving, anointed with a knob of anchovy butter and a squeeze of lemon.

Brussels Sprout

Brassica oleracea gemmifera

"The Cymae or sprouts rather of the Cole are very delicate, so boil'd as to retain their verdure and green colour. The best comes from Denmark and Russia . . ."
–John Evelyn, *Acetaria: A Discourse of Sallets,* 1699

*A*s previously mentioned, as a *Brassica,* Brussels sprouts are closely related to cauliflower, cabbage, and broccoli, and historically the entire crucifer clan was anciently and collectively referred to as the catchall "colewort"; so throughout their travels in Europe and, subsequently, the New World, there was often scant delineation. Many believe Brussels sprouts to be an ancient European crop, descended from the wild cabbages of prehistory and introduced into Belgium by Julius Caesar. Certainly the Romans were fond of a small, edible sprout they called *Bullata gemmifera,* or "diamond-maker," due to its purported ability to make you brighter. As well, *spruyten*

Brussels Sprouts 'Rubine'

32

were included in market regulations in Belgium and *spruyts* mentioned in English markets as early as A.D. 1213. There are also numerous sixteenth-century references to an edible plant known as *sproqs*, and John Evelyn's seventeenth-century *Acetaria* references "sprouts," although, again, whether these allusions can be pinned to the things we now know as Brussels sprouts remains in doubt.

Many contemporary botanists feel that the Brussels sprout is a mid- to late-eighteenth-century invention, and was perhaps a refinement of the small-headed Milan cabbage, cultivated by the farmers of the Low Countries and appearing on the vegetative scene after 1750. From this region it is believed by this faction that they then spread to France and England in the early nineteenth century, and finally to America and Thomas Jefferson's kitchen garden at Monticello in 1812.

However, there are those who dispute even this cultivar's Flemish origin, holding that the common name derives from the nineteenth-century forms most available in Europe, which happened to originate with growers near Brussels. What does seem to be beyond doubt is that the historic coleworts that ultimately led to the development of what we now know as the Brussels sprout were selected over the centuries in whatever country in which they found themselves to achieve their current tall profile and uniform, walnut-sized "sprouts." I hope all this information is sufficient to making the historical roots of this handsome vegetable perfectly clear.

Basically, Brussels sprouts, as members of the *Brassica* family, are tiny cabbages that grow along a stout, upright stalk and, stature-wise, along with the artichoke and cardoon, are certainly one of most impressive presences in the vegetable garden as well as being mightily commendable for their healthy doses of vitamin C, beta-carotene, and cancer-inhibiting agents. Some of the most popular contemporary cultivars are the regulation green 'Diablo', 'Dimitri', 'Jade Cross', 'Long Island', and the lovely purple-tinged varieties 'Rubine' and 'Falstaff.'

Culturally, all Brussels sprouts are extremely long-season vegetables, clocking in at anywhere from 90 to 150 days, and, ultimately, each plant will need a 2-foot-square area in which to grow. Also, do keep in mind that sprouts that have been exposed to one or more solid frosts are infinitely sweeter than not, so this is definitely a late-fall crop. Therefore, start plants indoors in early summer, transplant out mid-summer and plan on harvesting late fall or even out of the snow. Sprouts don't appear until the plant has reached its full stature, then start ripening from the bottom up; so in terms of harvesting, begin picking at the bottom, breaking off the leaf below the sprout, then removing the sprout. The upper sprouts will continue to mature as the lower ones are harvested.

Serve these little beauties by simply incising an X in the base of each, lightly steaming (don't overcook!), then tossing with pine nuts and some fried slivered pancetta and its renderings.

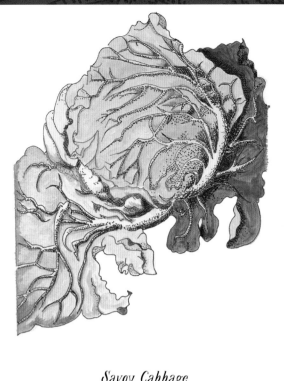

Savoy Cabbage

Cabbage

Brassica oleracea capitata

"But, after all, cabbage is greatly accus'd for lying undigested in the stomach and provoking eructations; which makes me wonder at the veneration we read the ancients had for them, calling them divine and swearing 'per brassicum."

—John Evelyn, *Acetaria: A Discourse of Sallets*, 1699

*A*s we have discussed in the two previous chapters, the family of coleworts is as wildly diverse and incestuous a group of vegetables as you will happen upon, with countless varieties and a whole host of disguises. Many believe that the oldest crucifers were wild mustards and that non-heading cabbages and kales were probably the first to be under domestication by the Celts sometime before 1000 B.C. Cabbage appears to be a later iteration of this far-flung dynasty, the *oleracea* affixed to the "armed" *Brassica* due to the controversial smell of this genus, *oler* translating to "odor" in Latin, and *capitata* added in tribute to the cabbage's "head"-ing growth habit. It seems cabbages first appeared in England in the fourteenth century, where they were called *caboches,* from the old French; they were sufficiently ubiquitous in France by 1420 that the anonymous *Journal d'un Bourgeois de Paris* reported "the poor ate no bread, nothing but cabbages and turnips . . . ," and they were ultimately introduced to the American continent by the French explorer Jacques Cartier in 1541.

In ancient Rome, grated cabbage was regularly applied as a poultice for sores and tumors and, in his *De Agri Cultura* of about 160 B.C., Cato the Elder held the interesting notion that disease could be prevented by bathing in the urine of cabbage eaters. By the first century A.D., the eminent Roman agriculturist Columella, in his *De Re Rustica,* was commending it, raw and pickled, for its effectiveness in counteracting the effects of alcohol. In fact, the Greeks, Romans, and Egyptians, in general, believed that wine and cabbage were natural opponents in the battle for sobriety and that the latter, being a heartier, brawnier sort, would claim the laurels if consumed in sufficient quantity. John Evelyn apparently concurred with this estimation, though not without reservation, in his *Acetaria* of 1699, reporting that "in general, cabbages are thought to allay Fumes and prevent intoxication: but some will have them noxious to the sight . . ."

Cabbage 'Ruby Ball'

By 1885, the illustrious French seed house Vilmorin-Andrieux was listing 68 different varieties of cabbage in its seminal *The Vegetable Garden,* and today there are hundreds of cultivars coming to us from all corners of the globe, all to be envied for their impressive vitamin C and K content. The three main types are the familiar dense, bowling ball–like green varieties, the deep red/purple varieties, which are true powerhouses of vitamin C, and the prettily crinkled, mild-flavored Savoys. The Oriental napa cabbage and that host of *chois* (Japanese for "vegetable") are also relations serving to round out the international selection.

Cabbage is a hardy, cool-season crop that does best under uniformly cool, moist conditions, so start indoors 4 weeks before last frost and plant out early, or direct sow in late June and thin to 18 inches to allow the heads to form during the cool of fall. They will prefer a sunny, well-drained loam soil that's been amended with some organic matter but will do fine in even mediocre soil. However, it's important to never grow cabbage or any other *Brassica* in the same soil more than once every three years (and to keep soil pH above 6.8) to avoid the dreaded club root, a fungal disease of which, I assure you, you want no part. On the farm, we like the lovely, crumpled heads of a Savoy type cut into thick wedges, braised in chicken stock, then tossed with a dollop of sour cream and some cumin and coriander.

Carrot

Daucus carota sativus

Carrots were so highly valued as an aphrodisiac in ancient Rome that the decidedly bent Emperor Caligula invited the entire senate to dine and fed them a banquet composed solely of carrot cuisine, so that he might observe them "rutting like animals."

Carrots are so unbelievably old that fossil pollen dating from the Eocene Epoch (a mere 55 million years ago) has been identified as belonging to a member of the carrot family. Most historians believe the carrot originated in what is now Afghanistan, although ancient seeds have been found as far afield as the prehistoric lake dwellings in Switzerland and the eighth-century B.C. Hanging Gardens of Babylon. Egyptian tomb paintings dating to 2000 B.C. frequently portray a plant now thought by many experts to be a purple carrot and, today, wild carrots can still be found growing throughout Europe, Western Asia, Afghanistan, and Turkey. By the eighth century A.D., the French Emperor Charlemagne was growing carrots in his imperial potager, by the thirteenth, the carrot had set roots in India and the Far East, by the fourteenth, was under cultivation in the Netherlands and Germany, by the fifteenth in England, and by the very early sixteenth, carrots had found their way to the New World. However, as with some other contemporary food plants, the ancient Greeks and Romans rarely

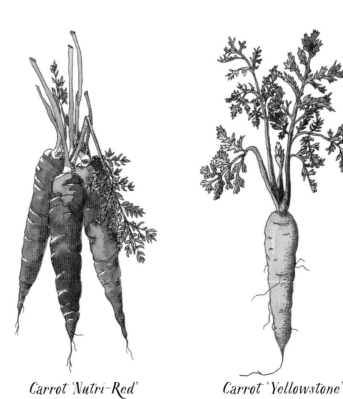

Carrot 'Nutri-Red'   Carrot 'Yellowstone'

Carrot 'Thumbelina'

ate carrots, employing them instead for medicinal purposes ranging from poultices for ulcerous sores to prescription as both a stomach tonic and eyesight enhancer. Dioscorides, botanist to Nero, writing in the first century A.D., reported, "Ye root ye thickness of a finger, a span long, sweet-smelling . . . is good for . . . ye bitings and strokes of venomous beasts . . . and . . . the leaves being beaten small with honey, and laid on, doth cleanse rapidly spreading destructive ulceration of soft tissues." As in early Rome, carrots were also broadly popular as a love potion with the ancient Greeks, who called the root Philon or Philtron from the Greek word *philo,* meaning "loving." What we know for certain is that carrots are excellent sources of beta-carotene, fiber, vitamin K, and potassium, and the important antioxidants carrots contain can protect against heart disease, cancer, and cataracts, inhibit tumor growth, and even retard premature aging.

During their long history, carrots appeared in an astounding range of hues, from purple, green, red, and black to pale yellow and white. In fact, one the few colors carrots did not seem to come in was orange. Bizarrely, the familiar orange root was first bred by the fastidiously patriotic Dutch, who, crossing pale yellow types with anthocyanin-rich red ones in the sixteenth century, refined cultivars to grow in the heraldic color of their ruling House of Orange. And though that familiar long, orange Bugs Bunny of a carrot surely reigned supreme for most of the past centuries, in recent years multihued carrots, particularly of the yellow, red, and purple varieties have made a comeback, as well as diminutive orb-shaped cultivars like 'Thumbelina', which are perfect for dense soils.

Most carrots will thrive in any sunny spot with deep, moist, sandy soil to allow for uninterrupted root growth. Direct sow seeds in early spring, thinning to 1 inch apart, and you should be harvesting these robust roots in about 74 days. In terms of culinary employment, why not follow the example of England's Elizabeth I, who, when presented by the Dutch ambassador with a tribute of a diamond-studded wreath of carrots and a tub of butter from Holland, plucked off the diamonds and rushed the carrots and butter off to the kitchen, giving birth to the classic dish of boiled, buttered carrots. Add a sprinkle of chopped, fresh dill to give it a regal touch all your own.

Cauliflower

Brassica oleracea v. botrytis

"Training is everything. Cauliflower is nothing but cabbage with a college education."

—Mark Twain

As I have noted ad infinitum, cauliflower, as a member of the *Brassica* family, is an extremely intimate relation to broccoli, the two cousins being so incestuous that those shadowland broccoli varieties broccoli 'Romanesco' and "broccoloflower" share the same botanical variety, *botrytis,* with cauliflower, deriving from the Greek meaning "cluster." The word *cauliflower* is a marriage of the Latin *caulis* for cabbage and *floris* for flower and, as such, the intricately wrought cauliflower has always been considered the beauty of the clan.

Many believe its original home was the isle of Rhodes, and the oldest known reference to cauliflower dates from the sixth century B.C. Pliny the Elder wrote of them in the first century A.D., and they were known in Syria before the twelfth century A.D., the Arab botanist Ibn al-'Awwam of that era referring to them as "flowering Syrian cabbage," and by the end of the twelfth century, at least three varieties were described in Spain as recent introductions from Syria. By the beginning of the sixteenth century, cauliflower had spread to Turkey and Egypt, then into the southern basin of the Mediterranean, Italy, and finally most of Europe by the end of the sixteenth century. In England, by 1586, cauliflower was enthusiastically offered for sale as "Cyprus colewort," suggesting introduction from the island of Cyprus, and English herbalist John Evelyn opined in 1699 that the best "cauly-flower . . . comes from Russia and Denmark." They were introduced into France from Italy in the sixteenth century, Olivier de Serres reporting in his *Théâtre de l'Agriculture* of 1600 that "cauli-fiori . . . as the Italians call it, . . . are still rather rare in France; they hold an honorable place in the garden because of their delicacy," and the cauliflower made its way to Haiti as early as 1565, finally finding its way to the New World with the earliest slave trade. By the late nineteenth century, as many as a dozen varieties of cauliflower were offered by American seed houses.

Aside from that familiar white curd cluster prevalent in our markets, like the carrot, a bevy of alternate hues have entered the fray of late, including orange, green, and deep purple varieties, the latter being the result of a purple-hued mutant discovered in a field in the late 1980s and years of classical breeding at the Hans Henrick Breeding Station at Danefield in Denmark. As with both red cabbages and wines, the gorgeous burgundy-violet coloration is due to anthocyanins, those mighty antioxidants we should all be consuming in quantity; so while the white types are good for you, the purple types, including modern varieties like 'Purple of Sicily' and 'Graffiti Hybrid', are excellent for you. The green types include the gorgeous 'Romanescos', and the modern orange cultivars, which contain 25 percent more vitamin A than the white varieties, are usually of a 'Cheddar' classification, although not at all cheesy.

Cauliflower 'Purple of Sicily'

All crucifers are cool-weather vegetables, and cauliflower is more sensitive to hot weather than most, so it will do best when daytime temperatures are between 65 and 80 degrees and it's set out as a 4- to 6-week-old transplant rather than planted from seed. All will grow well in any reasonably fertile, well-drained soil and are frost tolerant; so for a fall crop, set out transplants around July 1, spaced 14 to 20 inches apart. Harvest the curds before the buds begin to separate, about 2 months after transplant, cutting each head so that at least two wrapper leaves are present for optimum flavor. I've always thought the sweet, nutty flavor of cauliflower is wonderfully enhanced as they prepare it in India: simmered with potato, onion, and broth into a fragrant and savory vegetable curry.

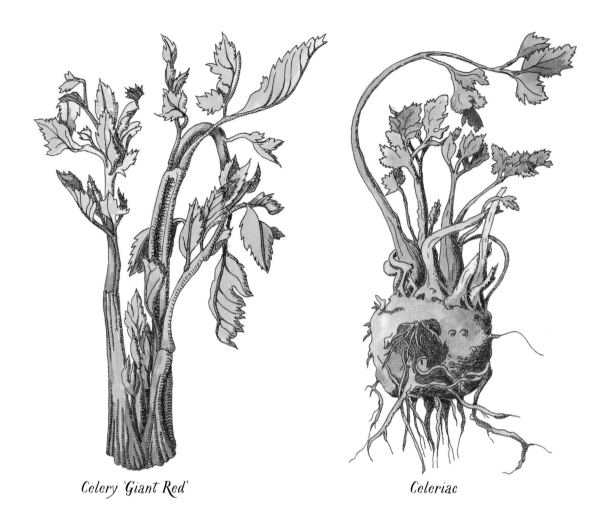

Celery 'Giant Red'

Celeriac

Celery

Apium graveolens

*"Sellery ... for its high and grateful Taste, is ever plac'd
in the middle of the Grande Sallet at our Great Men's Tables and
Praetor's Feasts as the Grace of the whole Board."*
—John Evelyn, *Acetaria: A Discourse of Sallets,* 1699

*O*ur modern-day celery is a descendant of the wild celery, also called "meadow parsley" or "smallage," which can still be found growing in marshy locales all over Europe, the Caucasus, and Asia Minor, and there is still some confusion surrounding the roles of those *Apiaceae* cousins celery and parsley in early history. For one thing, their leaf shape is remarkably similar, so whether the plant portrayed in Egyptian tomb paintings, including those embellishing the final resting place of Tutankhamun, is parsley or wild celery is still a source of debate. Additionally, *celery* derives from the French *celeri,* which comes from the Italian *seleri,* which, in turn, derives from the Latinization of the Greek *selinon,* which was the Greek word for parsley. So when Homer refers to horses grazing on selinon in the *Iliad* and fields of violets and selinon in the *Odyssey,* to which food plant is he actually referring? The oldest known usage of the word *celeri* occurs in a ninth-century poem of obscure French or Italian origin in which the plant's medicinal merits were positively articulated, including popular employment as a laxative, diuretic, cure for jaundice, and as a poultice for the bites of "wild beastes."

We now know that although celery is not a vitamin powerhouse, it is extremely low in calories, being, basically, fiber and water, and does contain a battery of good-for-you phytonutrients. Selection of the wild plant for medicinal purposes began in Italy in the sixteenth century, then in France as a kitchen herb later in that century, where it managed to gain some reputation as an aphrodisiac, Mme. de Montespan, mistress of Louis XIV and mother of seven of his children, having made *soupe de celeri* an integral part of the intimate dinners she held at court. By the middle of the seventeenth century, the stalks and leaves were being commonly consumed in both countries, and four varieties were reported under cultivation in Europe's North American colonies by 1806.

In fact, there are three basic types of celery: stalk, or "Pascal" celery (v. *dulce*), the familiar, crunchy green sort; golden self-blanching, or leaf celery (v. *secalinum*), grown for it aromatic foliage and seeds; and celeriac, or celery root (v. *rapacium*), cultivated for its tasty, knobby root. Some of the currently popular Pascal sorts are 'Conquistador', 'Monterey', and 'Utah'. 'Safir' is the most popular leaf variety, and 'Giant Prague' and 'Brilliant' are the currently favored celery root cultivars.

In terms of culture, the Pascal types are, to be brutally honest, finicky sorts, insistent on cool-ish temperatures and a steady supply of water to not turn overly fibrous and bitter, and, additionally, most clock in at 100 days plus from planting; so if your zone is prone to long, hot summers, celery success may be somewhat elusive. However, if you are determined to give it a try, start seeds in trays 6 weeks before your frost date and plant out about the first of June, spacing plants a good 12 to 14 inches apart. Leaf celery will be a kinder choice, as fibrousness is not an issue, and celeriac is another long-season water craver but not such a stickler for cool temperatures: therefore start seeds indoors 2 months before your frost date, transplant out just after last frost 10 inches apart, and harvest the roots when baseball sized.

Culinarily, I like braising the Pascal types in butter and a good beef or chicken stock, and celery root is heavenly mashed with half as much potato, butter, cream, and a drizzle of truffle oil.

Chamomile

Matricaria recutita, Anthemis nobilis

"Like a chamomile bed,
The more it is trodden
The more it will spread."

—Ancient English verse

This is a two-for-one idea, as here unfolds a Prince and the Pauper–like story of dual, nearly identical protagonists, each, as in Mark Twain's tale, being hailed by various national clacks as the "true" variety and one routinely being mistaken for the other. On one hand, there is what we call "Roman" chamomile *(Anthemis nobilis),* an aromatic creeper originally native to the Mediterranean and southwest Asia, the "Roman" idea having been bestowed upon it in 1598 by Joachim Camerarius, the German humanist and scholar, who observed it growing in profusion near Rome. On the other hand, there is the "German" chamomile *(Matricaria recutita),* a sweet-scented plant native to the European continent and western Asia, in this pretender's case, the *Matricaria,* thought to derive from *matri caria,* "beloved mother," in reference to St. Anne, the mother of the Virgin, to whom this plant is dedicated.

German Chamomile   *Roman Chamomile*

German Chamomile   *Roman Chamomile*

Chamomile comes to us from the Greek *khamai,* "on the ground," and *melo,* "apple," thus "ground apple," referring to Roman chamomile's low-growing habit and apple-like scent, Pliny the Elder describing the plant as having the aroma of "apples or quinces." Roman chamomile is the "true" chamomile of the British Isles, constituting one of the early Saxons' nine sacred herbs. *Matricaria recutita,* the German chamomile, is held by its supporters to be the "true" chamomile of continental Europe and is also widely naturalized in the United States.

The truth is that there are marked similarities between these two claimants to the true chamomile crown – such as fine, feathery green foliage and white daisy-like flowers with yellow centers – the main difference being their growth habits: Roman chamomile is a perennial and forms a dense, scantily blossomed low mat, while German chamomile is an annual (although happily self-seeding), with a looser, multi-branch and blossom clumping habit to about 2 feet.

Just to confound matters further, the chamomiles, while being profoundly different in chemical components, were almost identically employed herbally, having been used as "strewing" herbs, sleep aids, treatments for fevers, colds, and stomach ailments, complaints "of the mother," and as anti-inflammatories, as well as externally as a compress for sciatica, gout, lumbago, rheumatism, and skin ailments. On the continent, German chamomile was so highly prized as an herbal remedy in its namesake country that it earned the title *alles zutraut,* meaning "capable of anything." The American Dr. W. T. Fernie, in his *Herbal Simples* of 1914, referring to the Roman variety, maintained that "no Simple in the whole catalogue of herbal medicines is possessed of a quality more friendly and beneficial to the intestines than Chamomile flowers." Research has confirmed many of the traditional uses of these plants, and chamomile is included in the pharmacopoeias of twenty-six different countries, and is still widely employed as an antipeptic, antispasmodic, antibacterial, antifungal, and antiallergenic idea. Additionally, the Herb Research Foundation in Boulder, Colorado, estimates that, worldwide, over a million comforting cups of chamomile tea are consumed each day, making it the most widely consumed of all herbal teas.

As noted, Roman chamomile is perennial, easy to propagate from seed and hardy to USDA zone 3. For lawns of this summer-flowering herb, space plants 12 inches apart and tread them in firmly: just as in the old verse, it will not only not hurt them but will make them root better. German chamomile is sown (or self-sown) in spring or autumn and the flower heads picked when in full bloom in summer. In any case, do plant some of either variety, as both are lovely and health-giving plants. Dry some flower heads and render yourself a soothing cup of the most popular herbal infusion in existence.

Chard

Beta vulgaris cicla

"It grew with me in 1596 . . . which plant nature doth seeme
to play and sport herselfe: for the seeds taken from
the plant, which was altogether of one colour and sowne, doth bring
forth plants of many and variable colours . . ."
—John Gerard, *The Herball*, 1636

A member of the *Beta vulgaris* family, chard is a distant cousin of those other "greens"
spinach and orach, and a kissing cousin of the beet. Now, let's get the Swiss-
ness issue out and over once and for all. The hard fact is, chard isn't any more native
to Switzerland than, say, the palm tree. Clocks, yes. Intractable neutrality, surely. But

chard? Not on your retentive timetable. One erstwhile theory has it that it was one of two botanists, either the Swiss Gaspard Bauhin in the sixteenth century or the German Karl Heinrich Emil Koch in the nineteenth, who authored this cultivar's common name, and since either of those times, the name has stuck. In truth, the original home of chard most probably lies considerably farther south, in the Mediterranean region, as its culinary and medicinal virtues were lauded by Aristotle himself as early as the fourth century B.C. However, oddly, there is scant other historical mention of this handsome and healthy food plant, contemporary Mediterranean cuisine expert Clifford Wright citing for this omission the enormous number of aliases by which it was known; for instance, in English alone: "white beet, strawberry spinach, leaf beet, Sicilian beet, spinach beet, Chilian beet, Roman kale, and silverbeet." Adding to the confusion, chard has always presented itself in a good number of colorful disguises, Gaspard Bauhin, who might be the author of that "Swiss" idea, recording white, yellow, red, and "dark" varieties in his *Phytopinax* of 1596. By 1636, however, English herbalist John Gerard had definitely identified "chard" and continued to note of it that "the leaves . . . are for the most part very broad and thicke, like the middle part of the cabbage leafe, which is equal in goodnesse with the leaves of the cabbage being boyled."

Chard is also one of the healthiest vegetables on earth. A single cup of cooked chard contains 636 percent of your daily dose of vitamin K (important for maintaining bone health), 60 percent of your allotment of vitamin A, 42 percent of vitamin C, and 38 percent of magnesium; yet it contains a paltry 35 calories. Its fortifying combination of nutrients and fiber also seems particularly effective in preventing digestive-tract cancers, precancerous lesions in animals having been found to be significantly reduced following diets heavy in chard extracts.

As noted, there are many fine and colorful varieties available, from yellow-ribbed 'Canary' chard and pink-ribbed 'Flamingo Pink' chard to orange-ribbed 'Oriole', crimson-ribbed 'Ruby', and that some-of-each seed collection known as chard 'Bright Lights', so why not plant one of those vs. the relatively lackluster white-ribbed varieties? Chards are a relatively carefree thing to grow: start in seed cups 4 weeks before last frost and plant out, or direct sow after danger of frost ½ inch deep, 2 to 3 inches apart, in well-dug, fertile soil (optimum soil temperature for germination is 55 to 75 degrees). Thin to 8 to 10 inches apart after plants reach a height of 3 inches, and enjoy the show.

I'm very fond of making a summer relish with the colorful midribs of these beauties (reserve the leaves to sauté as spinach). Cut stems into medium dice, braise covered in a bit of olive oil with diced onion, golden raisins, a minced garlic clove, and a pinch each of brown sugar, cumin, and cardamom; then toss with freshly chopped mint, cool, and enjoy.

Cherry

Prunus cerasus, Prunus avium

*In a reversal of the typical journalistic "hatchet job," the tale
of our first American president's inability to tell a lie is,
in fact, a fabrication concocted by Parson Mason Locke Weems
in his overly laudatory Washington biography of 1800.*

Cherries are believed to have originated in the area between the Black and Caspian seas in Asia Minor in about 4000 B.C., then entered the Middle East by the third millennium B.C.; from there, many believe it was birds that carried cherry pits into Europe prior to even human civilization, *avium,* the sweet cherry's subgenus being Latin for "of the birds." The English word *cherry* originates in the Assyrian *karsu* and the Greek *kerasos,* which also gave birth to the sour cherry's current subgenus sobriquet *cerasus.* Pliny the Elder reports eight varieties being cultivated in Italy by the first century A.D., also mentioning cultivation as far north as Great Britain by that same date. Then, bizarrely, during the Dark Ages, the art of their cultivation in northern Europe seems to have been misplaced altogether, and the cherry had to be reintroduced into England in the sixteenth century by that famous gourmand Henry VIII. By 1640, however, more than two dozen cultivars were recorded there, many imported to the New World by the first Massachusetts Bay colonists in 1629.

There are two main types: the sweet cherry, *Prunus avium,* eaten right off the tree, and the sour, or "tart," cherry, *Prunus cerasus,* which is used almost exclusively for pie filling. Upon their introduction into the New World, sour cherries seemed to do admirably, especially as they continued their journey westward to the middle of the continent and the Great Lakes region in the late eighteenth century. Sweet cherries, however, refused to prosper in the hot humidity of the eastern United States and did not find a truly accommodating home until they were delivered to the Pacific Northwest in the early nineteenth century.

Sour cherry cultivars are divided into two main groups: the "Amarelles," identified by their vigorous, upright trees, pale or reddish fruit, and low acidity, and the "Morellos," characterized by small, bushy, compact trees, dark red fruit, and higher acidity. Some of the most popular cultivars are 'Montmorency', 'North Star', and 'Early Richmond'. Sour cherries are also nicely self-fertile and bear later than the sweet types, which makes them infinitely more frost resistant. Sweet

Cherry 'Montmorency'

cherries are self-incompatible, so cross-pollination by at least two varieties will be essential. Some to consider in this tasty group are 'Bing', 'Lambert', and 'Rainier'.

Cherries are chockablock with nutrients, including the important antioxidants beta-carotene and quercetin (which also provide significant anti-inflammatory relief for gout sufferers), and pectin, that cholesterol-lowering soluble fiber, as well as impressive doses of vitamin C, sour cherries having almost double the amount as the sweet types. Additionally, it is really hard to beat a cherry tree in blossom. Therefore, why not give one (or two) a try?

In general, it is wise to keep cherry trees pruned to about 12 feet for ease of picking, and spaced 20 to 30 feet apart for optimal sunlight and airflow. Excellent crops can be expected from both types after about 5 years, after which trees will remain happily productive for 25 years or more.

In the case of the sweet cherry, I advise grabbing a handful right off the tree. As for the sour types, how about a basketful in a chilled summer soup? Boil a pitted pound of them in 1½ quarts water with ¾ cup granulated sugar till soft, then whirl it up in the blender with a cup of sour cream, a pinch or two each of salt, confectioners' sugar, and flour to thicken slightly; chill and serve to sundry gasps of delight.

Chervil

Anthriscus cerefolium

*"Cherville ... with other Herbs are never to be
wanting in our Sallets ... being exceedingly wholesome
and chearing to the Spirits."*

–John Evelyn, *Acetaria: A Discourse of Sallets,* 1699

Native to the crags of southern Russia and the Middle East, and a close cousin to both carrots and parsley, true chervil *(Anthriscus cerefolium)* is not to be confused with either sweet chervil *(Scandix odorata)* or Spanish chervil *(Myrrhis odorata),* also known as sweet cicely, both of which bear a resemblance to it and share its anise-like scent and savor.

A basketful of suitably venerable chervil seeds dating to the fourteenth century B.C. was unearthed from Tutankhamun's tomb, but, oddly, there is negligible mention of chervil in ancient Egypt. It was the Romans who first carried chervil into Europe, ultimately delivering it into France in the first or second century A.D., where it found a happy, mainly culinary home. Interestingly, chervils (although this reference is clearly originally linked to Spanish chervil) were once collectively referred to as myrrhs, as the scent of their volatile oil was thought to resemble that of the resinous myrrh so

Chervil

48

Chervil seed

famously delivered to the Christ Child by Balthazar, purported king of either Arabia or Ethiopia, on Christmas Eve. Because of this olfactory connection, chervil became closely associated with Easter and the Resurrection, and it is still traditional in many countries to serve chervil soup on Maundy Thursday in commemoration of the Last Supper.

Pliny the Elder commented in the first century A.D. that "chervil was a fine herb to comfort the cold stomach of the aged," and Nicholas Culpeper similarly reported in the seventeenth century that "the garden chervil doth moderately warm the stomach . . . it is good to provoke urine, or expel the stone in the kidneys, to send down women's courses and to help the pleurisy and prickling of the sides." John Gerard, somewhat less enthusiastic, warns in the same century that chervil ". . . has a certain windiness, by meanes whereof it provoketh lust." The "chearing" property noted by John Evelyn was also a common herbal assertion, folk medicants throughout Europe maintaining that a cup of chervil tea would bestow good humor, sharpened wit, and even youth upon the lucky consumer. We know now that the active constituents of chervil include bioflavonoids, which aid the body in the absorption of vitamin C; and, for the most part, modern herbal medicine concurs: chervil is a "warming herb" that can help stimulate the appetite, act as a mild diuretic, and aid in digestion.

There are two main types of true chervil: plain and curly, both being hardy annuals featuring lacy parsley- or carrot-toplike leaves, pretty, small, white, parsley-like umbels, and growing to about 2 feet. Chervil both grows and goes to seed quickly, especially in hot weather and, unlike most herbs, will prefer a cool, shady spot in your garden as well as regular watering. Additionally, chervil does not take well to transplanting, so seed in place, thinning plants to about 10 inches apart. Chervil matures in about 6 weeks, so succession planting will be of the essence, and keeping the leaves pinched back to prevent flowering and seeding will not only promote bushier growth but will also help retard the "going to seed" idea.

Chervil has a famously subtle but immensely refreshing flavor that hints of licorice and is an essential ingredient in the classic French *aux fines herbes*. Here, however, I will pause to recommend an ancient herbal treat: brew a spot of chervil tea with a spoonful of the chopped fresh herb, let it steep for 20 minutes, cool, moisten two cotton balls with a bit of it, and place over tired eyes for 10 minutes – infinitely refreshing.

Chives

Allium schoenoprasum

*"I confess I had not added these had it not been
for a country gentleman, who by a letter certified to me that
amongst other herbs I had left these out."*

–Nicholas Culpeper, *The Complete Herbal*, 1653

Despite Culpeper's somewhat pouty inclusion of chives in his *Herbal* of 1653, I personally cannot think of a tastier culinary herb that provides such a pleasing and carefree show. Members of the *Allium* family, along with garlic, onions, leeks, and shallots, chives are the smallest species of onion and the only *Allium* native to both the New and Old Worlds, growing wild across most of the northern hemisphere, from Greece to the south of Sweden on the European continent, in Siberia as far east as Kamchatka, and broadly in North America. Chive cultivation in China dates back to possibly 3000 B.C., with Traditional Chinese medicine anciently recommending raw chives as an antidote for poison, and chives have been cultured in Europe since at least the Middle Ages, with many attributing their introduction there to Marco Polo.

The species name *schoenoprasum* derives from the Greek *skhoinos*, "sedge," and *prason*, "onion," which in Latin translates to "Rush-Leek." This onion cultivar's common name comes to us from the French *cive*, which derives from the Latin *cepa*, "onion." While in ancient Rome it was believed that chives could relieve the pain of both sunburn and sore throat, increase blood pressure, and act as a diuretic, they were not without their naysayers, the clearly wary Culpeper further asserting, "If they be eaten raw . . . they send up very hurtful vapours to the brain, causing troublesome sleep and spoiling the eyesight . . ." Therefore, chiefly valued as a sallet herb, even this usage was met with some suspicion, William Rhind reporting in his *History of the Vegetable Kingdom* of 1842 that ". . . they seldom find a place in the garden of the English peasant, who, partly from ignorance, and partly from prejudices, does not live much upon these soups and savoury dishes . . ." In truth, the medicinal properties of chives, which contain allyl sulfides and alkyl sulfoxides, as well as healthy doses of vitamins A and C and calcium, are similar to those of garlic but proportionally weaker. Therefore, while not wildly efficacious, chives can certainly have a beneficial effect on the circulatory system and in lowering blood pressure, as well as serving as an antibiotic due to their load of sulfurous compounds.

Chives

As noted, chives, with their tasty green stalks growing as elegantly as a decorative grass and topped with those lovely purple or white edible allium flower heads, are exceptionally decorative, particularly as a border plant for a vegetable or herb garden, functioning as both an ornamental edging and opportune pest barrier. Additionally, chives are positively lamblike to cultivate – perennial, hardy to USDA zone 3, and uncomplaining in sun to part shade and almost any soil. Chives can easily be grown from seed, but the best way to increase your holdings is to divide and conquer: just dig up a clump, tease the bulblets into several smaller clumps, and replant. Cut back chives after flowering to about 2 inches above ground, and they will reward you with new growth and another pretty flurry of flowers.

In his 1806 book *Attempt at a Flora,* Anders Retzius, the nineteenth-century Swedish anthropologist, describes how chives were broadly used in Sweden to add a green bite to pancakes, soups, and fish. I recommend chopping a bunch into a confetti, then sprinkling liberally over mashed potatoes, stirring into classic vichyssoise, or whipping into an omelet batter and freezing the rest (they remain wonderfully fresh tasting) to thaw at a later date when some summery "green" addition is all you crave.

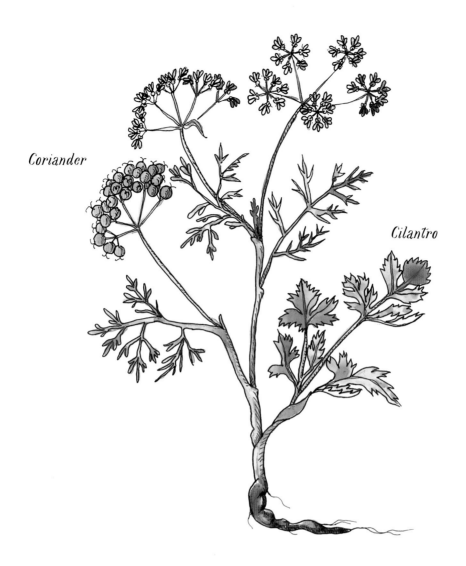

Coriander

Cilantro

Cilantro (Coriander)

Coriandrum sativum

"And the house of Israel called the name thereof
Manna: and it was like coriander seed, white; and the taste
of it was like wafers made with honey."

–Exodus 16:31

Call out the botanical psychoanalysts, as this is a clear case of horticultural identity crisis. In this "two faces of herb" scenario, "cilantro" and "coriander" are the personas in question – but they are one and the same plant. Another lacy, prettily umbled member of the greater carrot family, properly, the plant and "seeds" (actually the fruit) of *Coriandrum sativum* should be identified as "coriander," while the leaves alone constitute what we know as "cilantro."

Coriandrum sativum was anciently cultivated by a host of notable early civilizations, remains having been excavated from the Pre-Pottery Neolithic B level (9600-8000

B.C.) of the Nahal Hemar Cave in Israel, an Early Bronze Age site (3500-2000 B.C.) at Sitagroi in Macedonia, and the tomb of Tutankhamun (1324 B.C.) in Egypt. Additionally, it is one of the bitter herbs ordained by Jewish tradition to be eaten at the Passover feast. Due to cilantro's somewhat controversial scent (*coriander* coming to us from the Greek *koris*, signifying "bedbug," as the unripened seeds and leaves were thought to be fragrantly similar to that unpopular nocturnal companion), it is interesting to note that it was reportedly introduced into northern Europe by the Romans for its ability to make spoiled meat palatable by masking the rotting aroma of the *viande* in question.

Herbally, it was mainly coriander seeds rather than cilantro leaves that found wide-

Coriander

spread medicinal employment, the Egyptians, Greeks, and Chinese all believing that coriander had important aphrodisiacal properties. The ancient Egyptians also brewed *Coriandrum sativum* tea to treat urinary tract infections and headaches, and employed the crushed seeds and leaves in poultices to relieve the symptoms of rheumatism. Still other early physicians recommended ingesting coriander to combat flatulence and aid in digestion, and Hippocrates touted it as an effective "aromatic stimulant." Modern medicine confirms that coriander and cilantro are wonderful sources of dietary fiber, manganese, iron, magnesium, vitamin C, vitamin K, protein, and a host of phytonutrients, making it very good indeed for helping to lower both bad choles-terol and blood sugar, promote liver and nervous system function, and doing triple antioxidant duty as an anti-inflammatory, anti-septic, and anti-carcinogen.

An easy-to-culture annual, *Coriandrum sativum* does not take well to transplanting, so sow seeds in situ in a well-lit position in your garden when weather has warmed up (remember, this is a Mediterranean native), ultimately thinning to about 4 inches apart. The only slight downside to this piquant food plant is that it is prone to going to seed, which is happy news if it is coriander you are after and slightly tiresome if it is the cilantro leaves you cherish. In any case, sow every 3 weeks or so and you should be nicely supplied with both all summer long. Harvesting leaves should be fairly apparent. Harvest coriander seeds by cutting the stalks after they have fruited, bundling them, and then drying upside down in a paper bag. Give the bag a few brisk shakes to separate seeds from chaff.

Coriander seeds are generally toasted before use to bring out their spicy, citrus-like flavor, and they are wonderful combined with cumin and cardamom in Far East Indian cuisine. Cilantro, of course, is what makes guacamole sing, so I believe it would be churlish to recommend anything but a classic guacamole here. Therefore, coarsely mash two ripe avocados with a handful each of chopped tomato, onion, and cilantro, a diced jalapeño, the juice of a lime, and a good pinch each of salt and black pepper. Grab a tortilla chip and bully your way to the front of the line.

Cranberry

Vaccinium macrocarpon

*"It has been an unchallengeable American doctrine
that cranberry sauce, a pink goo with overtones of sugared
tomatoes, is a delectable necessity of the
Thanksgiving board and that turkey is uneatable without it."*

—Alistair Cooke (1908-2004)

The "American" cranberry *(Vaccinium macrocarpon)* is native only to North America, but, being the largest-fruited of all cranberry varieties, has been naturalized to many parts of the globe. Known by a host of Native American names, it was the earliest European settlers who coined the term *crane berry*, as it was thought the cranberry's small pink blossom resembled the head and bill of a crane. Native Americans employed the cranberry in myriad valuable ways, including as a natural carmine dye, mashed into a poultice to draw poison from arrow wounds, and, famously, pounded into venison to create their long-keeping dried pemmican, the cranberry's natural benzoic acid content preserving the meat almost indefinitely. The Delaware Indians of New Jersey, who called it *pakmintzen*, were so fond of the cranberry that they revered it as an earthly symbol of peace and plenty, and, of course, the Pilgrims were legendarily served cranberries by the hospitable Wampanoags at their first Thanksgiving meal in 1621. As well, because of their impressive vitamin C content and storability, barrels of cranberries could be found onboard nearly every eighteenth-century American sailing vessel as an extremely effective preventative against scurvy.

The American cultivated cranberry industry saw its birth in 1816 in Dennis, Massachusetts, when Captain Henry Hall noticed that the sand blowing in from the beaches onto his bogs improved his wild cranberry production dramatically. Hall subsequently began transplanting wild cranberry vines into manageable beds, and then topping them off with sand, a technique that soon gained mass popularity. Oddly, for a useful food plant, the cranberry is still surprisingly untamed, most modern varieties having been delivered directly from the wild. There are more than 100 varieties of these cranberries growing in North America, mainly in Massachusetts, Wisconsin,

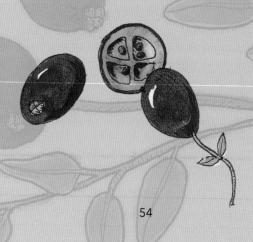

54

Cranberry

Oregon, and Washington, the historic favorites being 'Stevens', 'Early Black', 'and 'Howes'. However, in 1994, researchers at the University of Wisconsin succeeded in hybridizing 'HyRed', the first new publicly available cranberry in more than three decades. Not only ripening a full two weeks earlier than its parent 'Stevens', 'HyRed' also produces berries containing three times the anthocyanin as its antecedent, making every berry an antioxidant powerhouse. As well, like all cranberries, 'HyRed' is nicely high in vitamin C, relatively low in calories, and a good source of fiber and potassium. So, while any cranberry will be good for you, why not head directly to 'HyRed' if you choose to culture some?

I would hazard to guess that most people are unaware of the ornamental value of the cranberry as an extremely appealing low-growing ground cover. Hardy to zone 2 south to Virginia and west to Indiana and Michigan, the American cranberry, in general, boasts small, handsome, evergreen leaves that, when planted at 1-foot intervals, will grow into a solid, 10-inch-high thatch of pleasing deep greenery. Additionally, their pretty white-to-pink flowers will bloom in June and July, followed by the familiar, supremely decorative red fruit in fall. Contrary to popular misconception, cranberries do not need or even care for "bogs." What they prefer is an acid peat soil with a top dressing of sand (although they will grow perfectly well in ordinary garden soil), plenty of sun, and regular watering. With proper care, cranberries can produce for 100 years or more, and one 5-foot-square patch will reward you with up to 5 pounds a year of fruit once established.

Despite Alistair Cooke's uncharitable pronouncement, I suggest making the simplest of cranberry sauces by boiling 2 parts cranberries to 1 part each water and refined sugar until suitably thickened.

Cress

Lepidium sativum, Rorippa nasturtium-aquaticum

"Of darting fish, that on a summer morn
Adown the crystal dykes of Camelot
Come slipping o'er their shadows on the sand . . .
Betwixt the cressy islets, white in flower."

–Alfred, Lord Tennyson, "Geraint and Enid," 1859

We will be discussing here not one but two cresses coming to us from entirely different botanical families and each dwelling in that horticultural shadowland between vegetable and herb, or what the sixteenth-century English herbalist John Evelyn would term a *sallet*. Although there are others, the cresses that will capture our attention here are the common garden cress *(Lepidium sativum),* indigenous to western Asia, and watercress *(Rorippa nasturtium-aquaticum,* also known as *Nasturtium officinale),* native to Eurasia. Both are generally consumed fresh and green and both are prized for two important commonalities, the first being their signature peppery bite, which, historically, was both an affordable and locally culturable alternative to *Piper nigrum* (black pepper), Philip Miller, founder of the Chelsea Physic Garden, commenting in the *Gardener's Dictionary* of 1768 that "the leaves have often been used by the country people to give a relish to their viands instead of Pepper, from whence it had the appellation of Poor Man's Pepper." Also notable is their shared vitamin and nutrient content, historically thought to boost brain power, an ancient Greek proverb urging, "Eat cress, and learn more wit."

Garden Cress

Watercress

The Persians and Cypriots seem to be the first to record the culture of garden cress. By A.D. 380, it was listed as a food plant of consequence by Palladius, Roman author of *De Re Rustica*, and, by A.D. 800, it had made its way into Charlemagne's list of useful plants, the *Capitulare de Villis*. According to Rhind's *A History of the Vegetable Kingdom* of 1865, garden cress was delivered into England in about 1548, and by the same century, all three varieties, 'Common', 'Broad Leaf', and 'Curled', had been identified.

Garden cress is nicely low in calories but pleasingly high in minerals and vitamins, particularly vitamins A, B, C, and E, so sow seeds of any of these three every two weeks or so to enjoy a spicy supply all summer. A familiar denizen of cool flowing streams and stiller aquatic surfaces, watercress has been considered a purifier of the blood, a tonic, and a general revitalizer since it first extended its fresh greenery above an antediluvian surface, therapeutic employments running the gamut from treating head colds and digestive ailments to combating wrackings of the nervous system and improving bad complexions. It was recommended by Xenophon, the fourth-century-B.C. Greek historian, to be fed to children in order to improve their minds, and Xerxes, the Persian king of the same century, commanded its consumption by his soldiers for its health-giving benefits. Nicholas Culpeper rather snippily informs us in 1653 that "watercresse . . . is a good remedy to cleanse the blood in spring . . . and consumes the gross humours winter has left behind: those that would live in health may use it if they please, if they will not, I cannot help it." Watercress, in fact, is an excellent source of vitamins A, C, and K, potassium, iodine, iron, copper, and calcium, and its chlorophyll-rich leaves make it powerfully antioxidant.

Therefore, as it is currently naturalized through much of the United States, if you have a gently running stream near you, go find some watercress, dig up wads of it, and pop them into your local muck; otherwise, purchase some at your local market and compose a classic watercress sandwich to gobble at tea time: process a stick of butter with chopped watercress, lemon juice, and black pepper, slather on a slice of crustless white bread, add a fresh sprig of watercress, and top with another slathered slice.

Cucumber 'Painted Serpent'

Cucumber

Cucumis sativus

*"The fruit ... made into a potage with oatmeal ... doth
perfectly cure all manner of sauce flegme and copper
faces, red and shining fierie noses as red as red roses, with
pimples, pumples, rubies and such like precious faces."*

–John Gerard, *The Herball*, 1636

Cucumbers are among the most ancient of vegetables, having been thought to have originated in northern Africa, then traveling along the silk and spice routes north and west into Hindustan and Asia. The excavation of the famous Spirit Cave along the Myanmar/Thailand border in 1970 yielded a trove of cucumber seeds carbon-dated to an extraordinary 9750 B.C., and they were among the vegetables the Jews lamented leaving behind when they were expelled from Egypt. Cultivated cucumbers were certainly known in Italy by the second century B.C., when Marcus Terentius Varro gave this fruit the Latin name of *Curvimur,* referring to the usual curvature of its form. Tiberius, emperor of the Roman Empire from A.D. 14 to 16, famously demanded cucumbers year-round and had them grown in movable frames that could be positioned for optimal warmth and sun exposure. In France, the cucumber was listed in the *Capitulare de Villis* in the eighth century A.D., when it was a favorite of the Emperor Charlemagne, and it was most probably introduced into England in the fourteenth century during the reign of Edward III. Somehow, it seems, the cucumber was then misplaced by the English during the War of the Roses but was happily reintroduced there during the reign of Henry VIII with the advent of the Spanish-born Catherine of Aragon, who liked them in her salads. Columbus introduced the cucumber to Haiti in 1494, just fifteen years later Hernando de Soto reported seeing them in Florida, and in 1535, the French explorer Jacques Cartier found "very great cucumbers" growing on the site of what is now the modern city of Montreal.

In a typical early dichotomy of herbal opinion, the early Greeks named the cucumber *sikys,* signifying that the plant sadly lacked aphrodisiac qualities, while old English herbals recommended that any woman who wished for children should wear a cucumber strategically suspended from her girdle. In truth, while the cucumber is not a raucous bundle of healthfulness, being 95 percent water and offering up a small percentage of vitamin K, as John Gerard attested, it's a wonderful soother of skin complaints, and the contemporary beauty community still employs cucumber extracts in a wide variety of skincare products.

There are three main varieties of cucumber: slicers, which tend to be longer, smoother, more uniform in color, and thicker of skin than the other types; picklers, which tend to be shorter, thicker, less regularly shaped, and have warty skins; and burpless, which are sweeter, boast thinner skins, and are generally seedless. In terms of laudable varieties, there are many, ranging from the popular slicers 'Marketmore', 'Olympian', and 'Greensleeves' to the pickling cultivars 'National Pickling', 'Saladin', and 'Excelsior' and the burpless varieties 'Orient Express', 'Sweet Slice', and 'Armenian'. Start all cucumbers indoors 4 to 6 weeks before your frost date, then set out, with an absolute minimum of root disruption, only when soil temperatures are above 65 degrees and night temperatures won't dip below 60 degrees. A floating row cover will dissuade most of the early pests, and training cucumbers up a trellis as they begin to flower (they're terrific climbers) will help them grow straight and make them far easier to pick. You should be sampling most in 50 to 65 days. I recommend peeling, seeding, and cubing them, then tossing with yogurt, fresh pepper, chopped mint or cilantro, and a squeeze of lemon. The result is a coolly refreshing West Indian raita, the perfect accompaniment to a piquant chicken or lamb dish.

Currant

Ribes vulgare, R. nigrum, R. rubrum, R. petraeum, R. sativum, R. ussuriense

*Scottish lore held that good fortune would surely follow if, after
the wedding ceremony, in an apparently ancient show
of "tough love," the mother of the bride met her at the door and
broke a currant bun over her head.*

Confusion has hounded this berry-bearing family historically, as the true currant (*Ribes* spp.) became incorrectly commingled with the Zante grape *(Vitis vinifera)*, generally exported from the Greek city of Corinth and known continentally as Raisin de Corauntz because of their physical similarity when dried. Corauntz somehow managed to attach itself to the grape's dried Ribes double and, however erroneous, the name stuck.

Ribes, native to the northern hemispheres of most continents, counts the European red, pink, and white currants *(R. rubrum, R. petraeum, R. sativum,* and *R. vulgare)* and the European and Asian black currants *(R. nigrum* and *R. ussuriense)* among its constituents. The German-Swiss naturalist Conrad Gesner was known to have transplanted a variety of *Ribes petraeum* in his garden in 1561, and the British herbalist William Turner said of the currant in 1568, "Ribes is a little bushe . . . and in the tops . . . are red berries in clusters in taste at the first somethinge sower but pleasant enough when they are fully ripe." In the seventeenth century, however, John Gerard noted the black currant's "stinking and somewhat loathing savour," clearly in reference to this type's famously unaromatic foliage, thought by non-devotees to be regrettably redolent of cat pee.

Currant 'Titania'

Currant 'Pink Champagne'

However, it's the United States that really turned against the *Ribes* clan with bizarre gusto, for, after their introduction with the earliest English settlers and enjoying considerable popularity for both their medicinal and culinary merits, at the turn of the twentieth century, they were unjustly accused of spreading white pine blister rust *(Cronartium ribicola),* a disease lethal to five-needle pine trees. By 1912, both federal and state restrictions had been placed on their import and culture, and by 1920 an all-out federal ban been placed on black currants. And while the federal statute was rescinded in 1966, restrictive laws remain on the books in eleven states to this day. And, just to add another dash of contrariness to this agricultural maelstrom, in the United States, black currants have historically run a distant fourth in popularity behind the other varieties due to their unpleasant scent and exceptionally tart taste, John Hedrick, author of *Small Fruits of New York,* reporting in 1925, "Few Americans born in the country have tasted the fruit or, ever having done so, care for a second taste."

Here, however, let us remember that black currants offer twice the antioxidancy of blueberries, four times the vitamin C of oranges, and twice the potassium of bananas, and currants of any hue are excellent sources of vitamin C, fiber, and iron. Some of the most popular modern cultivars are the black currants 'Titania' and 'Ben Sarek', the reds 'Rovada' and 'Tatran', the white variety 'Blanka', and the gorgeous pink variety 'Pink Champagne'. Currants are basically native to cool-weather climes and will sulk and swoon in extended high temperatures and humidity, so all will enjoy part shade and a good layer of mulch to keep their feet cool. Also, a good fall pruning to selected second- and third-year canes will not go unrewarded. As all currants contain a number of tiny seeds, the best place to start for a fresh currant recipe is with strained juice. Therefore, clean 2 pounds of currants, remove stems, steam for an hour to extract about 5 cups, re-boil with a cup of sugar and a quarter cup lemon juice, mix 1 part juice with 3 parts water or seltzer, and serve refreshingly over ice.

Dill

Anethum graveolens

*"Trefoil, vervain, John's wort, dill,
Hinder witches of their will."*
—Sir Walter Scott, *Guy Mannering*, 1815

*A*nother member of the *Umbelliferae* (parsley) family, and indigenous to the Mediterranean, southern Russia, and western Asia, dill comes to us from the Old Norse *dylla*, meaning "to soothe" or "lull," dill being anciently prescribed to quiet colicky babies. Prescribed as a painkiller in the *Ebers Papyrus* of about 1550 B.C., dill was also employed by Hippocrates in a decoction for cleansing the mouth, and ancient Greco-Roman soldiers applied the burnt seeds to their wounds to promote healing. In his *Second Eclogue* of about 35 B.C., the poet Virgil speaks of dill as "a pleasant and fragrant plant," and Pliny lauded dill's curative powers in the first century A.D. Intriguingly, dill was a potent ingredient of both beneficent wizardry and black witchcraft in the Middle Ages, as noted by the Elizabethan poet Michael Drayton in his 1629 *Nymphidia, the Court of Fairy*, when he reports, "The nightshade strews to work him ill, / Therewith her vervain, and her dill." Dill, however, was also a common charm against witchcraft, as witnessed by Meg Merrilies' incantation over the crib of Henry Bertram in Sir Walter Scott's *Guy Mannering*, and it was also held that, should a witch darken your doorway, the offering of a cup of dill tea would rob her of her ill will.

As early as the eighth century A.D., Charlemagne was serving bowls of dill at his banquet tables so guests who overindulged might benefit from its carminative properties, and this anti-"windinesse" idea was one that has followed dill about for centuries, the anonymously authored British *Banckes' Herbal* of 1525 stating that "dill assuageth wicked winds in the womb [stomach]," and Nicholas Culpeper writing with signature bluntness in 1653, "The decoction of Dill, be it herb or seed . . . is a gallant expeller of wind . . . ," further commenting, "The seed, being roasted or fried . . . dissolves the imposthumes in the fundament," which, I am certain, will make all of us rest more easily tonight.

We know now that dill's health benefits are the product of two components: monoterpenes and flavonoids. One of the monoterpenes, carvone, has a discernable calming effect on the stomach and aids in digestion by relieving intestinal gas. Contemporary German tests also confirm that dill's essential oil relaxes the smooth muscles that

Dill

control intestinal motility, thus reducing colicky abdominal pain. Additionally, dill's volatile oils are known to help neutralize particular types of carcinogens, and dill is an abundant source of calcium, 3 tablespoons of the seed containing as much as a cup of milk.

An annual plant growing to about 30 inches, with signature feathery leaves, handsome yellow umbels, and pungent seed, distinctively aromatic dill is nearly unique in that both its leaves and seeds are used culinarily. Two excellent types are the familiar 'Dukat', with its tall, sturdy habit and large flower heads, and 'Fernleaf', a lovely dwarf variety perfect for use as a border plant. Dill loves a well-drained soil and plenty of sun and dislikes transplanting, so sow in situ; but it is otherwise a carefree sort, the only glitch being that it bolts easily in the heat and, once it sets seed, will die back in the typical life cycle of annual herbs. Therefore, sow dill spring to midsummer in batches and keep moist when young and you will have an ample supply all summer.

Both dill leaves and the dried seeds have that unique "dill" savor reminiscent of caraway and fennel: a sprinkling of freshly chopped dill leaves in a homemade chicken salad or over a plate of vinegared sliced cucumbers is surely a summer treat not to be missed.

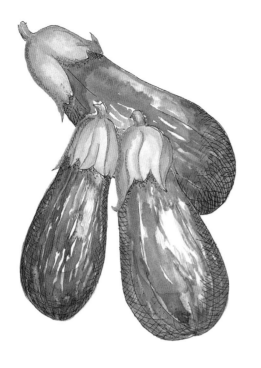

Eggplant 'Zebra Hybrid'    *Eggplant 'Neon'*

Eggplant

Solanum melongena

*"I think of the hundreds of poems of the eggplant & my friends
who have fallen in love over an eggplant, who have opened the
eggplant together & swum in its seeds, who have clung in the egg
of the eggplant & have rocked to sleep in love's dark purple boat."*

–Erica Jong, "The Eggplant Epithalamion"

Due to its membership in the highly suspect *Solanum* family as well as the bitter taste of its earliest incarnations, the eggplant has, historically, been one of those vegetables forced to wage a long and arduous battle towards gastronomic acceptance. Because of its *Solanum* roots and, therefore, close kinship to nightshade, the eggplant was known across many early cultures as the "madde" or "rage" apple, and, consequently, was thought to induce madness and even death. Additionally, because eggplants were believed to have originated near the Dead Sea and the imagined site of Sodom and Gomorrah, they were also known popularly, or perhaps unpopularly, as "apples of Sodom." Josephus, the ancient Jewish historian, wrote that he had himself seen the beautiful purple "apples of Sodom" which, magically and clearly with divine purpose, vanished in smoke when they touched one's lips. This bit of ancient lore was also employed by John Milton in *Paradise Lost*, when he spoke of the singularly disappointing diet of the fallen angels.

Interestingly, excavated remains have revealed that, very possibly, it was an invasive insect that begot this particular brand of heavenly magic, boring into the flesh of the eggplant and causing it to powder and decay interiorly while the skin remained beautifully intact. Thus, it would seem it was entirely possible to bite into what appeared to be a glossy bit of heaven only to come up with a mouthful of everlasting repentance. However, by the third century A.D., the eggplant's culinary competence was at least being entertained by the Chinese and, by the twelfth century, four varieties of this controversial plant were grown by the Spanish Moor Ibn al-Awwam, although it was still listed by Carl Linnaeus as late as 1753 as *Solanum insanum*.

The most common early type of eggplant was, in fact, a small, oval, white fruit so closely resembling a hen's egg that the genus, as a whole, assumed the name. Vilmorin-Andrieux listed this variety as "white eggplant" *(solanum ovigerun)*, describing it, however, as "more ornamental than useful," and further attesting that it was "considered by some to be unwholesome." Today, there are almost infinite varieties of eggplant in all kinds of shapes, shades, and dapplings, from the familiar Italian deep purple globe varieties like 'Florida Market', to the long, thin, Far Eastern types like 'Orient Charm' and 'Pintung Long', to the beautifully striated "graffiti" cultivars like 'Listada De Gandia', to the miniature varieties like 'Fairytale', 'Turkish Orange', and "Osterei', the latter being the hen's egg doppelganger.

All eggplants are desperate lovers of warm temperatures and grow best in full sun, so start indoors and transplant out when nighttime temperatures are consistently above 60 degrees, spacing plants about 15 inches apart. Regular watering will help avoid bitter-tasting fruit, and repeated harvesting will stimulate continuous production. At harvest, the skin of an eggplant should be taut and shiny; fruit that has lost its shine and begun to exhibit a bronze-y tone is overripe and most likely bitter.

In the kitchen, many chefs salt eggplant after slicing, allow it to drain in a colander, then rinse to remove any inherent bitterness. One of our favorite eggplant employments on the farm is a genuine Thai-style curry: cut the cultivar of your choice into cubes and sauté with a dollop of red curry paste and some cubed chicken breast, add a can of coconut milk, heat through, and serve atop some fragrant jasmine rice with chopped cilantro to garnish.

Eggplant 'Osterei'

Eggplant 'Turkish Orange'

Fennel

Foeniculum vulgare

"So Gladiators fierce and rude; mingled it with their daily food
And he who battled and subdued; a wreath of fennel wore . . ."

–Henry Wadsworth Longfellow, "The Goblet of Life," 1841

*F*ennel is native to southern Europe and southwestern Asia, although it is currently naturalized throughout northern Europe and much of North America and Australia. A member of the *Apiaceae* family (formerly *Umbelliferae*), *fennel* derives from the Latin *fœniculum*, meaning "small fragrant hay," purportedly for the warm similarity of its scent.

In Greek mythology, Prometheus employed a stalk of fennel to steal fire from the gods, this eventually translating to the ancient belief that the gods delivered knowledge to man in the form of a coal carried in a fennel stalk. The Greeks conquered the Persians at Marathon, or "place of fennel," in 407 B.C., Charlemagne declared fennel essential to every garden in A.D. 812, it is mentioned in Spanish agricultural documents of A.D. 961, and it was one of the nine herbs held sacred by the Anglo-Saxons, as noted in the *Lacnunga*, a tenth-century medical text, which recommends burning it as an inhalant for respiratory disorders.

It seems fennel managed to attract a lot of arcane associations during its long history, being aligned with flattery in Clement Robinson's *A Handful of Pleasant Delights* of 1584: "Fenel is for flatterers, an evil thing it is sure . . ." John Gerard noting in the sixteenth century, "The green leaves . . . or the seed . . . do fill women's breasts with milk . . . swageath the wambling of the stomacke, and breaketh the winde," and Nicholas Culpeper, in the seventeenth, lauding fennel's ability ". . . to provoke urine, and ease the pains of the stone . . . stays the hiccough, and takes away the loathings . . . ," as well as ". . . shortness of breath and wheezing . . ." In fact, the essential oil of fennel, rich in anethole and other terpenoids, has been proven to inhibit spasms in smooth muscles, contributing to fennel's use as a carminative, and is still included in a few national pharmacopoeias to treat chills and stomach ailments.

Fennel

Medicinal matters aside, visually and culinarily, fennel is a fantastic edible plant: exquisite of form with as sprightly a taste as dill or anise, whose licorice-like savor it shares, and the perennial sorts are surely worth a place in a decorative border. There are two main types: annual bulb fennel (*Foeniculum vulgare* var. *azoricum*), also called Florence fennel, grown for its crisp, anise-flavored bulb, and perennial herb fennel *(Foeniculum vulgare)* grown for its fragrant foliage and seeds. Some of the most stunning of the perennial variety (hardy to USDA Zone 4) are the gorgeous "bronze" types like 'Purpureum' and 'Rubrum', each growing to about 5 feet with clouds of feathery bronze-to-purple-toned leaves and umbels of pretty yellow flowers. Annual bulb fennel is a smaller, uniformly green variety, growing to 2 or 3 feet, two of the most popular contemporary cultivars being 'Trieste' and 'Perfection'. Florence fennel, harvested when the bulbs attain a 3-inch circumference, will crave even moisture, and a bit of hilling up when bulbs reach golf ball size to create a blanching environment will not go unrewarded.

To harvest the seeds (actually the fruit) of the perennial types, cut off the flower heads when the seeds turn brown, pop them into a paper bag, let them dry for a few days, shake the bag, remove the seeds, and store. In the kitchen, employ the tasty seeds in breads and meatloaves, the foliage of either variety to wrap and stuff a trout or other fresh catch for baking, and the bulbs sliced thinly with orange segments and dressed with a tart vinaigrette.

Fig

Ficus carica

*In 528 B.C., Siddhartha Gautama attained true enlightenment
and founded Buddhism while sitting under a fig tree.*

As every art historian knows, remove a fig leaf and uncover something sensational. Botanically, the fig may constitute the most remarkable form of fruit on earth, as it is not actually a fruit at all, but a hollow receptacle entirely lined with tiny flowers, which, in total darkness, manage to bloom and ripen seeds: that honeyed flesh is actually a miniature interior carpet of spent blossoms!

Both the Assyrians and ancient Sumerians coveted the fig as long ago as 2900 B.C., and figs were known in Crete by 1600 B.C. The early Greeks prized them so highly that in the original Olympic Games it was a fig leaf wreath rather than a laurel that crowned the victors, and Greek athletes supped almost entirely on figs, as it was believed they increased both strength and swiftness. In 717 B.C., Romulus and Remus, the fraternal founders of Rome, were said to be suckled by a she-wolf in the shade of an accommodating fig tree, and figs figured prominently in Homer's *Odyssey* as he narrates the agonies of Tantalus in the underworld: "Trees spread their foliage high over the pool and dangle fruits above his head . . . sweet figs and luxuriant olives." Figs are also mentioned extensively in the Bible, as in this passage from Numbers 20:5 concerning the flight of the children of Israel: "And why have you made us come up out of Egypt to bring us to this evil place? It is no place for grain or figs . . ." Pliny the Elder reports in the first century A.D.: "Figs are . . . the best food that can be eaten by those who are brought low by long sickness . . . They increase the strength of young people, preserve the elderly in better health and make them look younger with fewer wrinkles." Spanish and Portuguese missionaries imported figs into the Americas in the early sixteenth century, and the oldest living fig tree in the New World, the Pizarro fig tree, planted in 1538 by Francisco Pizarro, still stands at the governor's palace in Lima, Peru.

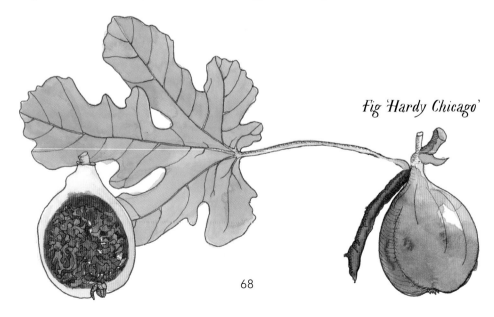

Fig 'Hardy Chicago'

Fig 'Petite Negra'

As you might have guessed, figs are, for the most part, temperate-to-subtropical plants, choosing to thrive best in hot, arid, Mediterranean conditions, but with the correct protection in winter, they can also prosper as far north as USDA zone 6b. There are both brown- and green-skinned varieties, the brown-skinned types like 'Hardy Chicago', 'Brown Turkey', and 'Celeste' being considered the hardiest. Green-skinned types include the popular 'Kadota', 'Sierra', and 'King', and both varieties will reward you with that uniquely delicious pink-to-strawberry-colored, honey-scented flesh.

If you are intent on culturing one in the ground, all figs will treasure a warm, sunny, protected spot in your garden and, certainly, in USDA zones 6 and below, heavily mulching and evenly "burying" your fig will be a worthwhile endeavor, burying entailing bending your tree to the ground, anchoring it, and topping it off with a fat layer of mulch. For less pliable models, an upright tarpaulin sheath stuffed with hay can also work. However, for most of you, I recommend doing as we do on the farm: pot up your fig in a substantial pot and when temperatures start to descend, wheel it into a dark space in which the temperature will not dip below 20 degrees (we put ours in our unheated garage), allow it to go dormant through the winter, then wheel it back out after danger of frost in spring.

Why not try any of these luscious beauties split, buttered with mascarpone, wrapped in a shred of prosciutto, and sprinkled with lemon juice and fresh ground pepper? Pure ambrosia.

Garlic

Allium sativum

"Without garlic, I simply would not care to live."
–Louis Diat, famed French chef and purported creator of vichyssoise

Botanists believe garlic originated in west-central Asia and southwestern Siberia, as garlic's wild cousin *Allium longicuspis* grows rampantly near Afghanistan's northern border and in the southern portion of the Ukraine. *Garlic* comes to us from the Old English *gar leac,* meaning "spear leek," and *Allium sativum* derives from the Celtic *allium,* "hot" or "burning," in reference to garlic's pungent personality, and the Latin *sativum,* "cultivated."

Archeologists have unearthed clay replicas of garlic bulbs from tomb sites at El Mahasna in Egypt dating to 3700 B.C., and Tutankhamun was sent on to the after-life accompanied with basketfuls in 1324 B.C. The builders of the pyramids were known to subsist almost exclusively on a diet of raw garlic and onions, and the Greek legions so famously consumed it to gird themselves for battle that, planting it wherever they conquered, they ultimately served to spread garlic throughout Europe. The Egyptian *Ebers Papyrus* of 1550 B.C. recommends garlic for 22 different ailments, the second-century B.C. Sanskrit *Charaka Samhita* applauds it for heart disease, rheumatism, digestive upsets, epilepsy, and leprosy, and the Talmud touts it as a sexual aid, urging men to eat garlic on Friday to prepare them for lovemaking on the Sabbath, when a bout of sheet-tossing was religiously encouraged. Garlic was one of 365 known plants cultivated medicinally in the Far East by 200 B.C., Pliny the Elder suggested it for 61 separate maladies in the first century A.D., and in the second century A.D. the Greek physician Galen dubbed it the "heal-all" of the people. Greek midwives habitually placed a necklace of garlic around a newborn's neck to protect it against ill humors, and in medieval Europe, braids of garlic were hung at the entrances of homes to ensure that evil and disease would not enter.

In 1858, it was none other than Louis Pasteur who ultimately proved garlic to be a supremely efficacious bactericide, a single milligram of raw garlic juice proving to be as effective as 60 milligrams of penicillin. British doctors characteristically applied a dilution of raw garlic to infected wounds during World War I, and Russian

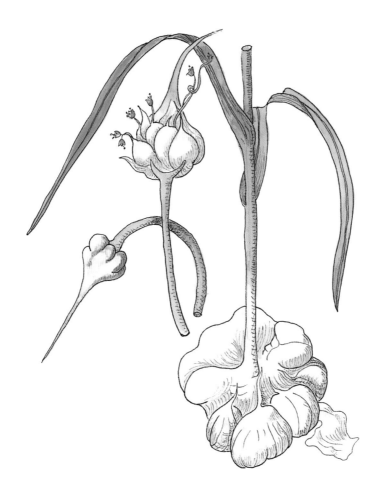

Garlic

army physicians employed the same technique in World War II. Additionally, garlic contains healthy doses of vitamins A, B, and C, and garlic's sulfur compounds help to regulate blood sugar, detoxify the liver, and stimulate both blood circulation and the nervous system.

There are literally hundreds of stellar varieties of garlic, including the hardneck 'Purple Stripe', 'Porcelain', and 'Rocambole' types and the softneck 'Artichoke' and 'Silverskin' varieties, coming to us from nearly every corner of the globe. Hardnecks will produce a "scape" around which the cloves cluster: a pretty, looping flower stalk prized for its subtle flavor when harvested in spring; soft-necks are stalkless and therefore more easily braided. My advice? Search out a couple of varieties that intrigue you in your favorite plant catalog, order some bulbs, divide them into cloves, and plant upright either in the fall or early spring an inch or 2 deep and 4 inches apart. For fall plantings in our cooler zones, be sure to mulch heavily to insure successful overwintering. Harvest mid to late summer when the leaves start to yellow, and hang them for a couple of weeks in a cool, dry place until the husks turn papery and they're ready to employ.

Here I will stop to recommend a roasted head squeezed onto some crusty French bread as a remarkably simple and healthful bit of kitchen alchemy: remove the papery husk, cut off top of the head to expose the meat of the individual cloves, slather with olive oil, and bake at 400 degrees for half an hour.

Goji Berry

Lycium barbarum

<blockquote>
*Chinese legend holds that one day a traveling merchant
who beheld a young woman whipping an ancient
gentleman, asked, "Why are you assaulting this old man?"
The lady replied, "I am disciplining my great-grandson."*
</blockquote>

Although its origins are murky (probably southern Eurasia), the *Lycium barbarum* has been employed in Traditional Chinese medicine for as long as recorded history. The young woman described above proved to be 300 years old, and when asked the source of her miraculous youth, she replied that the herb had many names and an application for every season: "In spring, take its leaves, known as 'essence of heaven' . . . In the summer, its flowers, known as 'longevity of life.' In the autumn, its fruits, known as 'goji berry.' In the winter, the bark of its roots, known as 'the skin and bone of the earth' . . . Take these four parts in the four seasons and you will have a life as lofty as heaven and earth."

Historically, the goji, or wolf berry, is also linked to the legendary emperor Shen Nung, father of Chinese agriculture and medicine, and to the potentially mythical Chinese herbal master Li Ching-Yuen, who supposedly married fourteen times, lived to the age of 197 (some disputed records suggest 252), and was known to consume goji berries daily. The seventh-century Chinese medical text *Yao Xing Lun* further maintained that the wolf, or goji, berry could "replenish the supply of body fluids, calm the spirit, refresh the skin, brighten the complexion, and strengthen the eyes," and the *Shi Liao Ben Cao* of the tenth century claimed that it "strengthens the muscles . . . prevents colds, and leads to longevity."

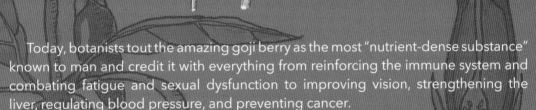

Today, botanists tout the amazing goji berry as the most "nutrient-dense substance" known to man and credit it with everything from reinforcing the immune system and combating fatigue and sexual dysfunction to improving vision, strengthening the liver, regulating blood pressure, and preventing cancer.

What modern science tell us is that gojis contain at least 6 vitamins (including C, B1, and B2), 18 amino acids, 11 essential minerals (including zinc, iron, copper, and calcium), 22 trace minerals, dozens of phytochemicals (including carotenoids, phenolics, and lycopene), and that in 2005 the goji's "Oxygen Radical Absorbance Capacity" (ORAC), which scores antioxidancy, received — at 30,300 TEs (micromoles of Trolox Equivalents per 100 grams) — the highest rating of any known food plant. Although further testing is necessary, in a recent Chinese study, a group of elderly patients were given doses of goji berry for three weeks, the highest percentage of them tripling their T-cell transformation functions and doubling the activity of their white cell interleukin-2. Additionally, a whopping 95 percent showed increased appetite and improved sleep function, and 100 percent demonstrated "significantly increased spirit and optimism."

Moreover, the goji is a hardy, unfussy brute: a thick bush reaching from 8 to 10 feet, withstanding winters down to -15 degrees F and summers above 100 degrees F, adapting to almost any sunny situation, and potentially thriving for several hundred years. In early summer, this unbelievably healthful food plant is laden with tiny, trumpet-shaped, purple and white flowers, followed in late summer by glossy, bright crimson gojis, and it will continue to both flower and produce fruit right up until heavy frost.

Honestly, fresh gojis are of variable savor, dependent on climate and soil, are difficult to harvest as they are notably easily bruised, and are historically shaken gently into trays and then slow-dried in the shade. For this reason, gojis are almost always found dried outside of their production regions, tasting much like raisins or dried cranberries, and are plentiful in health food stores, as are several varieties of goji juice drinks. My advice? Plant one, buy some, go forward — and prosper.

Gooseberry

Ribes grossularia, R. uva-crispa, R. hirtellum

An Old English wives' tale holds that one may cure a sty on the eyelid by pointing a gooseberry thorn at the unsightly blemish and chanting nine times in succession, "Away, away, away!"

Here we will weigh the merits of that *Ribes* constituent the gooseberry, which many botanists believe may even be primevally ancient due to the bristly fruit of the wildest sorts, and which numbers nearly 5,000 varieties. There are, however, *three* basic gooseberry types: the European gooseberries (*Ribes grossularia* and *Ribes uva-crispa*), the first being bristly skinned and indigenous to northern Europe, the second being smooth-skinned and native to the Caucasus, and the American gooseberry *(Ribes hirtellum)*, which is native to the north of the American continent.

Due to their affinity for cooler climes, their thorny, near-weedy ubiquitousness in their native habitats, and the uneven savor of their fruit, gooseberries achieved literally no botanical mention among the ancient Romans and Greeks. Their first mention in Europe takes place in England in 1276, when they were listed in purchases for the Westminster garden of Edward I, and it is in England almost exclusively that the fairly ignored gooseberry finally found a welcoming gastronomic home, John Gerard reporting in 1597 that "There be divers sorte . . . some greater, some lesse, some rounde, others long . . . These plants do grow in London gardens and elsewhere in great abundance."

Gooseberry 'Poorman'

74

By the mid-eighteenth century, culture of the gooseberry in home gardens in Great Britain became so popular that gooseberry clubs were formed, with members in fierce competition for the largest, meatiest fruit, culminating in the development of the massive 'London' gooseberry, which claimed the thorny crown for thirty-six years running. The large, sweet, green-skinned fruit most of us identify as the edible gooseberry is one of the European types, grown almost exclusively in England and rampantly prone to mildew in the United States. The American gooseberry, *Ribes hirtellum,* while better acclimated to our precincts, generally produces small, dark, almost inedibly tart fruit, and both types are possessed of a prickly demeanor famously daunting in terms of harvest, the English botanist John Parkinson commenting in 1629 that the plant was "armed with verie sharpe and cruell crooked thorns." Additionally, all gooseberries contain from 3 to 12 tiny seeds, which makes both processing and fresh eating a trial, and, as noted, many *Ribes* family members were banned entirely from culture in the United States for most of the twentieth century and are still illegal in some states. Is anyone still with me?

If so, as mentioned, there are scores of gooseberry varieties with varying personalities, from thorny to near thornless, small- to large-fruited, very tart to verging on sweetness, mildew and rust resistant to not at all, and in berry hues from yellow and green to pink and deep red. Some of the most popular American types are 'Captivator', 'Downing', 'Houghton', 'Poorman', 'Silvia', 'Welcome', and the nearly thornless 'Pixwell', and the European imports include 'Chataqua', 'Industry', 'Invicta', 'May Duke', and 'Whitesmith'. However, also as mentioned, the English types, while larger, sweeter, and tastier in the main, are also extremely prone to powdery mildew and other funguses, so forewarned is forearmed. As with all Ribes, cool temperatures, a good mulching, adequate air circulation, and some annual pruning to the strongest second-year canes will be rewarded.

And, as any gooseberry's complement of tiny seeds still makes them a culinary challenge, why not try them in a classic fifteenth-century Gooseberry Fool? Simmer 1 pound of berries, 1 ounce of butter, and 2 tablespoons of sugar over low heat until soft, mash enthusiastically, pass through a sieve, cool, fold in an equal amount of whipped cream, chill, and serve to gastronomic accolades.

Grape

Vitis vinifera, V. labrusca, V. rotundifolia

*"And Noah began to be an husbandman, and he planted
a vineyard: And he drank of the wine, and
was drunken; and he was uncovered within his tent."*

—Genesis 9:20-21

Piths of the wild *Vitis vinifera silvestris* have been found in Stone Age settlements from Germany to Cyprus, indicating consumption by Homo erectus pretty much since the dawn of time, and in the case of the grape, it seems nearly impossible to separate this ancient food plant from its fermented nectar, a wine jug unearthed in the northern Zagros Mountains of Iran dating to a impressively distant 5400 to 5000 B.C. During the Archaic Period in Egypt (c. 3100-2686 B.C.), pharaohs were buried with vast quantities of the nectar of the grape to slake their thirst in the afterlife, and in Late Uruk Mesopotamia (3500-3100 B.C.), it is known that at least the upper classes were enjoying wine with becoming regularity. In Greco-Roman myth, Dionysus was the Thracian god of wine, representing, among other fine things, wine's power to "liberate" oneself from restraint and self-consciousness — as we experienced in the 1970s, if this led to the dipping of a toe into the inviting waters of ecstatic and orgiastic excess, well, how liberating!

Grape 'Concord'

Grape 'Neptune'

On the other side of the traditional coin, the liquor of the grape has also played a showy role in both Jewish and Christian ceremony, in Jewish ritual, the Sabbath starting with a blessing chanted over a shared goblet of wine, and in the Christian faith, the "water into wine" idea not only constituting the first of Christ's miracles at Cana but also serving an important symbolic role, along with the host, as the Eucharistic "body and blood" offered to the faithful.

Medicinally, in addition to providing us with vitamin C and manganese, grapes are loaded with phytonutrients, ranging from carotenoids to stilbenes like resveratrol, which is found in great concentration in red varieties, the total number running well into the hundreds, making all grapes true antioxidant, anticarcinogenic and anti-inflammatory dynamos.

There are three main types of grape: *Vitis vinifera*, the ancient Eurasian variety, thought to have originated near the Caspian Sea in Asia Minor, and *Vitis labrusca* and *Vitis rotundifolia*, both notably antique American varieties, the *Vitis labrusca* type growing with such wild early profligacy from Canada south to the Carolinas that, in the tenth-century A.D., the Viking explorers named Canada "Vinland." *Vitis rotundifolia*, the culturally finicky yet very healthful muscadine grapes, are original to Virginia south to central Florida and west to Texas, and are rarely grown outside their native habitat.

In truth, there are so many varieties of grapes suitable for every climatic particularity and wished-for employment, from fresh eating to wine production, that it would be impossible for me to recommend a couple of varieties to all of you. Therefore, my recommendation is to consult your local USDA Extension for the best type for your zone and needs. Whatever your choice, it will probably arrive to you bare-rooted, so upon arrival, soak it in a bucket for a couple of days, trim to the strongest single cane, dig a hole in full sun large enough to accommodate a careful spreading of roots, spacing vines at least 6 feet apart, and do provide some stout trellising. Vines may be espaliered in a host of pretty ways to suit your aesthetic whim, but some hard pruning before growth starts in spring will not only create the unrestricted airflow necessary to prevent diseases but increase productivity as well. And to be able to stand in the scented, green shade of your own grape arbor and pop a fresh, cooling morsel of fantastic health into your mouth of an August afternoon? Well, just think about it.

Grapefruit

Citrus paradisii

*During the Great Depression, the U.S. Welfare Board
was besieged with complaints from citizens using
food stamps that they had cooked the unfamiliar grapefruit
for several hours and it was still too tough to eat.*

While there is no evidence of the grapefruit in the Old World or Asia, in the West Indies there are vast populations growing seemingly wild; so it is therefore believed the grapefruit is a recent debutante on the edible plant stage and was born there a scant three hundred years ago, most probably as an accidental mating of the pummelo (or pomelo) *(Citrus grandis)* and the sweet orange *(Citrus sinensis)*. The pummelo, native to Malaysia and Indonesia, was delivered into the West Indies from the Malay Archipelago by one Captain Shaddock, an English ship commander, in 1693, becoming known alternately as the "shaddock." The orange was introduced to the New World by Columbus in 1493, when he carried seeds into Hispaniola (Haiti). The English reverend Griffith Hughes chanced upon either the pummelo or the grapefruit in 1750 and, as he happened to be on a quest for the true identity of that pesky apple of Eden, decided to elect the large, yellowish, West Indian thing that he had discovered, naming it the "forbidden fruit," a designation which followed both the pummelo and grapefruit around for decades. In 1820, the Chevalier de Tussac, a French botanist, reported from Jamaica, "I have had the occasion to observe . . . a variety of shaddock whose fruits, which are not bigger than a fair orange, are disposed in clusters; the English in Jamaica call this the 'forbidden fruit' or 'smaller shaddock.'" Somewhere along the line, this "disposed in clusters" idea generated the grapefruit's present odd sobriquet, as nothing could be less grape-like than a grapefruit. The botanist James MacFadyen finally differentiated the grapefruit from the pummelo in his 1837 work *Flora of Jamaica,* and the grapefruit was delivered onto the American continent by Dr. Odet Phillipe, a French naval surgeon who settled at Safety Harbor, Florida, in 1823.

The first commercial grapefruit grove was established by John A. MacDonald in Orange County, Florida, in 1870, and the first exports from Florida to Philadelphia and New York occurred between 1880 and 1885. The pink grapefruit was born in Florida in 1907 as a renegade sport of the white-fleshed 'Walters' variety, and in 1929, a Texas breeder discovered a red grapefruit growing on a pink grapefruit tree and named it 'Ruby Red', it ultimately becoming the first grapefruit ever granted a U.S. patent as well as the official state fruit of the Lone Star state.

Therefore, contemporarily, grapefruits come in three basic descriptions: white, pink, and red, some of the most popular varieties being 'Duncan', 'Star Ruby', 'Foster', 'Marsh', 'Ruby Sweet', 'Oroblanco', 'Paradise Navel', 'Thompson', and 'Rio Red'. All grapefruits are high in vitamins A and C, a host of B vitamins, calcium, potassium, and magnesium, but it's the lycopene-rich pink and red types that really shine health-wise, and grapefruits, in general, are touted for their ability to stimulate digestion as well as for their diuretic properties. Additionally, grapefruits are really lovely trees with large, shiny, ovate leaves and fragrant, white, four-petaled blossoms; the trees will start bearing copiously about four years after planting, so if you are in USDA zone 9 or above, I say why not? For the rest of us, many types can be dwarfed with some energetic pruning and will do just fine in a ten-gallon pot to be hauled into the greenhouse or your sunniest window in winter.

In the kitchen, try whipping up a tangy grapefruit vinaigrette for your next salad by pureeing 1 cup chopped flesh with ½ cup water, ¼ cup cider vinegar, 4 tablespoons maple syrup, and a sprinkling of salt and pepper.

Grapefruit 'Rio Red'

Honeyberry

Lonicera caerulea v. edulis (Lonicera Kamchatka)

*One of the interesting residual benefits of glasnost, which
marked the restructuring of the Soviet Empire in 1986, was the
introduction of the Russian-bred honeyberry to the world.*

*A*lthough honeyberries are not currently commercially available except as plants, and that scarcely, many fruit growers are convinced that this tasty berry will be the broadly feted darling of both supermarkets and nurseries in the next decade. Highly valued in its native habitat of Transbaikalia, the mountainous region east of Lake Baikal in Russia, and in Japan, where is it known as Haskap, this "blue" member of the honeysuckle family was first mentioned as a food plant of interest in 1894. Champions of this sprightly berry decided its honeysuckle roots would impede commercial popularity, and so the *Lonicera caerulea* v. *edulis* ("edible blue honeysuckle") was rechristened "honeyberry" around the turn of the twentieth century. Not to be confused with either the Old World hackberry *(Celtis australis)* or the West Indian Spanish lime *(Melicocca bijuga),* both also known as "honeyberry," *L. caerulea* v. *edulis* is the only member of the "blue honeysuckle" clan that is edible. Although there are some eighteenth- and nineteenth-century references to an "edible, early-ripening wild berry resembling a blueberry" in Russian and Japanese texts, the historically "closed" societies of both of those nations, and particularly the Soviet Union in the twentieth century, made dissemination of any information concerning the development of the honeyberry extremely late in coming.

We know the first attempts to domesticate the honeyberry in Russia date to about 1913; however, really extensive work did not commence until the 1950s, when the Vasilov Research Institute in St. Petersburg and the Siberian Horticultural Institute in Barnaul plunged into honeyberry hybridization with a good amount of attention. It appears that *Lonicera caerulea's* most promising breeding cultivars hailed from the Kamchatka Peninsula of Russia (thus *Lonicera kamchatka,* the honeyberry's alternate botanical name), and collecting missions by the Vasilov Research Institute, conducted from 1972 to 1990, ultimately identified some 500 different edible honeyberry types.

The first three Russian hybrids to hit the market, 'Start', 'Goluboye vereteno', and 'Sinyaya Ptitsa', were released in 1980, and by 1998 the number of viable commercial cultivars offered for sale in Russia had grown to sixty. As well, culture of the Haskap in Japan, primarily on the island of Hokkaido, has yielded a booming modern commercial industry.

Visually (and, most feel, culinarily), the honeyberry does, in fact, resemble an elongated blueberry, dented at the nether end, the berries being produced on compact 5-foot shrubs in easy-to-harvest clusters, with each berry containing not only a tiny edible seed but a significant (think blueberry-like) load of antioxidants as well.

As you might expect from their points of origin, honeyberries are mightily hardy to USDA zone 3, and, even more impressive, honeyberries typically require only one growing season to fruit and the fruit is produced exceptionally early—about 2 weeks before the first strawberries appear. In terms of cultivar, there seems to be a "blue" theme running through the most popular, with 'Blue Belle', 'Blue Bird', 'Blue Forest', 'Blue Moon', 'Blue Pacific', and 'Blue Velvet' leading the pack, all offering attractive dark green foliage followed by delicate yellow/white flowers in early summer, with the deep blue berries arriving mid-summer, followed by very vivacious golden fall foliage. Honeyberries are also nicely uncomplaining in terms of soil preference, drought tolerance, pest issues, etc., but are not self-fertile, so it will require at least two varieties and some cross-pollination to have them fruit successfully.

Some people feel the honeyberry tastes of blueberry infused with black currant, so employ them deliciously every way you would a blueberry, including over your cereal at breakfast time, and have something horticulturally cutting edge to chat about at dinner.

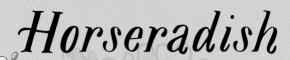

Horseradish

Armoracia rusticana

"The radish is worth its weight in lead,
the beet its weight in silver,
the horseradish its weight in gold."
—The Pythia (Delphic oracle) to Apollo, eighth century B.C.

A member of the *Brassicaceae* family and a cousin to all "cole" crops as well as the mustards, whose hot temperament and essential *oil (allyl isothiocyanate)* it shares, *horseradish* is believed to be a bastardization of the German *meerrettich*, or "sea radish" (*radish* from the Latin *radix*, for "root"), as it grew historically by the sea, the *meer* ("sea") then being manhandled to *mahre* ("mare"), thus "mareradish," and, finally, "horseradish." *Armoracia* also identifies a seaside habit: the Latin *ar*, "near," wedded to *mor*, "the sea."

Although originally native to Russia, Hungary, and western Asia, horseradish is one of the ancient bitter herbs celebrated in the Jewish Passover seder, Cato discusses it in his *De Agri Cultura* of the second century B.C., and it is most probably the Amoracia mentioned by Pliny the Elder for its medicinal virtues in his *Naturalis Historia* of A.D. 77. Horseradish figures in countless medicinal applications historically, John Parkinson stating in 1629, "The horseradish is used Physically, very much in Melancolicke, Spleneticke, and Scorbutic diseases." Nicholas Culpeper adjured that "the bruised root laid to the part affected with the sciatica, joint-ache, or the hard swellings of the liver and spleen, helps them all . . ." in 1653, and John Evelyn commended it as an "antiscorbutic" in 1699. The American herbalist William Thomas Fernie concurs with a number of these estimations in his classic *Herbal Simples* of 1897, stating, "The fresh root of the horseradish is a powerful stimulant, by reason of its ardent and pungent volatile principle, whether it be taken as a medicament or applied externally to any part of the body . . ." Modern science tell us, that horseradish's impressive vitamin C, mineral, and dietary fiber content and healthy battery of glucosinolates, like sinigrin, make it powerfully antioxidant, antibacterial, and anticarcinogenic.

Perennial to USDA zones 5 through 9 and easily grown as an annual in other zones, horseradish is a strikingly massive plant growing to about 3 feet, the two basic types being the wide, crinkly-leaved 'Common', or 'Maliner Kren', the variety generally available for cultivation in home gardens, and the 'Bohemian' types, including such cultivars as 'Bohemian Giant', 'New Bohemian', and 'Swiss', with smooth, tapered leaves and generally employed by commercial growers. A notable late-twentieth-century entrant into the horseradish arena is the 'Big Top Western' variety, bred for improved disease resistance, and also notable is the spontaneously cream-splotched beauty 'Variegata'.

Horseradish roots are generally planted in very early spring and harvested after a couple of touches of frost in late fall. Propagated by division when the root is dug up for consumption, the main root is harvested with one or two offshoots being replanted to produce next year's crop. Experts recommend planting roots at a 45-degree angle in well-dug soil leavened with a bit of compost and, once planted in any of our perennial zones, your stand will continue producing without complaint for years.

John Gerard observed in 1597 that ". . . the Horse Radish stamped with a little vinegar put thereto, is commonly used among the Germans for sauce to eate fish with and such like meates as we do mustarde . . . ," and it wasn't until the mid-seventeenth century that the British finally embraced horseradish as the consummate condiment to accompany an oyster or a classic roast beef. If you have never had your own fresh-grated horseradish, you are in for a treat: peel and cube the root, food process with a bit of cold water, then doctor with white wine vinegar and salt to taste.

Horseradish 'Variegata'

Huckleberry

Vaccinium spp. / Gaylussacia spp.

*According to The Guinness Book of Records, the world's oldest
living thing is a "box huckleberry" in Perry County, Pennsylvania, a
single plant spreading underground for almost a mile and being
believed to date to the eleventh century B.C.*

*T*his is the story of a fruit that simply cannot make up its mind, as there are "huckle-berries" belonging to three entirely different genera: *Solanaceae* ("garden huck-leberry"), *Vaccinium* ("bil-berry," "huckleberry," "farkleberry," "whortleberry," the latter, of course, to be wholly and historically confused with its "whortle" cousin the blue-berry), and that other *Vaccinium* relation in the greater *Ericaceae* family, *Gaylussacia* ("black huckleberry," "box huckleberry," "dwarf huckleberry"). The "garden huckle-berry," a *Solanaceae* relation of Deadly Nightshade, is entirely toxic and should be shunned outright. The related *Vaccinium* and *Gaylussacia* types boast both edible and nonedible varieties, a good number of which, as referenced, are called "huckle-berry," or some antique variation thereof. And, just to add one more stumbling block to this testy tale, in the United States, the edible *Vaccinium* types are native only to the Pacific Northwest, while the edible *Gaylussacias* are native to eastern America alone. Both wild *Vacciniums* and *Gaylussacias* (named for the nineteenth-century French physicist Joseph Louis Gay-Lussac) were an antique and important food source for a host of Native American tribes, in 1624, the Franciscan missionary Gabriel Sagard relating that the Hurons of the Great Lakes "... regularly dry them for the winter ... and that serves them for comfits for the sick," and Henry David Thoreau recounting that "... from time immemorial ... [Native Americans] have made far more extensive use of the whortleberry at all seasons and in various ways than we ..."

Huckleberry

The term *huckleberry* first appears in *The History of Carolina* by John Lawson, the surveyor general of that state, in 1709; they were an important part of Lewis and Clark's diet in 1805 and 1806; and, in 1868, Robert Brown, Scottish explorer of the Pacific Northwest, wrote of the scores of huckleberry cakes that could be seen drying in Native American villages "supervised by some ancient hag, whose hands and arms are dyed pink with them."

As mentioned, *Vaccinium* huckleberries are native only to the western United States and *Gaylussacias* to the East. In general, the *Gaylussacia* huckleberries are hardier (about zones 4 to 9), but the most common varieties, "dwarf," "box," "blue," and "black," are such touchy transplants and so readily available in the wild that they are virtually undomesticated. As for the *Vacciniums*, they are mostly only hardy to zones 7 through 9, although adaptable in terms of sun and siting, and have truly interesting landscape potential. Health-wise, all huckleberries of either genus, like all deep blue/black fruits, are loaded with healthful anthocyanins.

Here I will pause to bandy a few types about: *V. myrtillus,* native to both North America and Europe, is a handsome 2-foot bush, bearing flavorful ¼-inch black, purple, or dark blue berries; *V. caespitosum* is a wonderful ground cover growing to about 1 foot, with small, bright blue berries with excellent flavor; and *V. ovatum,* particularly the 'Thunderbird' variety, has a handsome upright habit to about 6 feet, especially attractive new red/bronze foliage, and tasty dark blue fruit that is both larger and bluer than most other types.

Would I honestly encourage you to plant a huckleberry? Let us put it this way: if you can make a 'Thunderbird' work in your environment, they are awfully decorative in a wet woodland setting. If not, there is undoubtedly some huckleberry or other growing wild in your precincts. Go taste one (not the *Solanum* variety!) and see if it is worth considering picking a bunch and stuffing them under a piecrust.

Kale 'Redbor'   *Sea Kale*

Kale

Brassica oleracea acephala, Crambe maritima

*The heirloom variety 'Jersey Kale' apparently reached such imposing
heights (to 9 feet tall) that its woody stems were traditionally
fashioned into popular and exceedingly well-priced walking sticks.*

*B*rassicas are a rather marvelous example of the natural law that holds that remarkable, even visionary discoveries can be made by simple, long-term, rudderless
refinement by people focused, merely and securely, on their own personal whims.
And these individual visions can be wildly diverse, which is why we count kale,
cabbage, kohlrabi, cauliflower, broccoli, Brussels sprouts, and all cress and mustards
as members of the *Brassica* family, descendants from what was probably a single wild
mustard of Mediterranean extraction. The distinguishing differences between these
plants are merely those introduced over the history of their selection by this or that
specific native preference. By the fifth century B.C., however, a predilection for ever
larger-leaved varieties led, from pretty much one end of Europe to the other, to the
development of the vegetable we now know as kale.

From visual evidence in such paintings as Pieter Bruegel's *The Numbering at
Bethlehem,* many botanists believe kale is the crucifer closest in appearance to that
original wild mustard ancestor, and because of its extreme cold-hardiness and cultural
adaptability kale was such an important food crop in Scotland, most Scottish homes
had "Kale Yards" – stone-walled, protective plots purpose-built to supply kale to both
man and beast through the winter, *The Edinburgh Testaments* of 1586 referring to
"Ane littill hous and cail yaird" and John Sinclair noting in his *General Report of the*

Agricultural State and Political Circumstances of Scotland in 1814, "Those who work as day-labourers, in the capacity of hedgers, ditchers, dikers, village-shoemakers, tailors, wrights or joiners, and the like, have now almost universally little gardens, called kail-yards, attached to them."

Add to that stoic cold-hardiness and general unfussiness the fact that one cup of kale will reward you with plenty of fiber, ten times your recommended daily dose of vitamin K, nearly 100 percent of your vitamin A, 71 percent of vitamin C, plus 45 different antioxidant and anti-inflammatory flavonoids and I believe were onto something.

Additionally, kales come in all kinds of decorative frillings and colorations, these coming from two main types: the 'Scotch Curled' and the napus, or 'Siberian', varieties. Some of the most popular 'Scotch Curled' types are the supremely frilly 'Vates Blue', the blue/green 'Winterbor', the deep red/purple 'Redbor', and the dramatically deep blue-green to almost black Italian heirloom 'Lacinato', also called 'Nero Di Toscana'. Some Siberian favorites are the beautiful white-veined 'White Russian', the 'Red Ursa', and the purple-veined, exceptionally hardy 'Winter Red'. Let me also just mention in passing here that tasty *Brassica* cousin Sea Kale *(Crambe maritima),* a perennial plant native to the sea coasts of Europe that, when sufficiently blanched and steamed, is consumed much like asparagus.

Kale is a fairly long-season plant and you will want to time its maturation with the advent of late fall, as flavor is always infinitely sweeter after a couple of real frosts. So count back about 80 days from the start of your frostiest (or merely coolest) season, and plant then: for instance, around mid-July where we are, spacing plants 14 inches apart in all directions.

Let us be blunt here: kale leaves can put the "rough" in roughage, so most leaves are best when small, before too much fiber develops; larger, tougher ones may be blanched briefly to tenderize before "raw" employment. In our neighborhood, kale chips are fast becoming the healthy snack du jour: remove stems and tear leaves into bite-sized pieces, lay on a baking sheet, sprinkle with salt and olive oil, and bake at 350 degrees until crisp, about ten minutes.

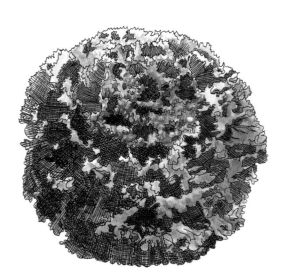

Kale 'Vates Blue'

Kale 'Lacinato'

Kiwi

Actinidia deliciosa, A. chinensis, A. arguta, A. kolomikta

*Due to its usually fuzzy and diminutively evocative form,
the French have attached the sobriquet souris vegetale to the
kiwifruit, translating to "vegetable mouse."*

The kiwi is a fruit so tardy to arrive on the world stage, it did not even acquire its current appellation until the middle of the last century. Born in the Yangtze River Valley of China, where, known as Yang-tao, it grew as wildly as kudzu does in the American South, girdling trees, swagging through forests, and generally growing so prolifically that the Chinese collected the fruit exclusively from the wild for several

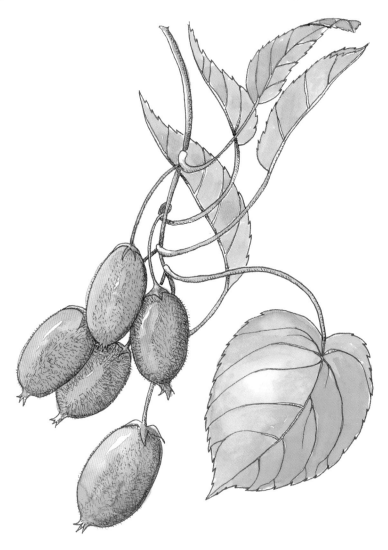

Hardy Kiwi 'Issai'

millennia. A member of the *Actinidiaceae* family, the kiwi has four main edible types suited from the most sweltering of climes to -30 degrees F: the small-fruited, mainly smooth-skinned *A. chinensis;* the familiar, larger, fuzzy-skinned *A. deliciosa; A. arguta,* the hardy kiwi, and *A. kolomikta,* the arctic kiwi, the latter two the result of breeding and selection for cold tolerance.

Then known universally as the "Chinese Gooseberry," the first kiwi to leave China is believed to be a hardy kiwi, carried home by Isabel Fraser, headmistress of the Wanganui Girls' College in New Zealand, from her sister's Chinese mission in 1904. In 1934, a kiwi vine introduced into the USDA Plant Introduction Station in Chico, California, thrived, becoming the single parent of the entire modern California kiwi industry, and, finally, in 1952, back in New Zealand, 13 tons of "Chinese Gooseberry" were exported to England, constituting the first-ever commercial kiwi shipment. It wasn't until 1959, that the Auckland fruit packer Turners & Growers decided to rename the fruit the more enticing "melonette," until they were apprised of the hefty import duties levied on melons, at which juncture they hopped right over to the Maori "kiwi," as the fruit was thought to resemble that round, brown native New Zealand bird.

Kiwis are one of the most nutritionally dense fruits in existence, with a battery of antioxidants, twice the vitamin C of an orange, 20 percent more potassium than a banana, and nice amounts of vitamin E, folic acid, and fiber. The University of Oslo reported that eating two to three kiwis a day will reduce blood clotting by an average of 18 percent and lower your triglycerides by an average of 15 percent, and the Rowett Research Institute in England found that your DNA repair rate nearly doubles with the consumption of kiwifruit.

There are about fifty varieties of kiwi ranging across the *Actinidia* family, the most familiar being the fuzzy, brown, commercially employed *A. deliciosa* cultivar 'Hayward', hardy to USDA zones 7 to 9. *A. chinensis,* or "golden kiwi," types have similar climatic boundaries, hardy kiwis like 'Anna', 'Geneva', and the self-fertile 'Issai', all fuzz-less and approximately grape-sized, are hardy to zone 4, and the arctic types like 'Arctic Beauty', the male cultivar boasting dazzling pink-and-cream splotched leaves, are amazingly hardy to USDA zone 3.

To say that kiwis are vigorous would be just touching on their profligacy, so some pruning and tying up of whatever cultivar works in your precincts will keep your glorious, jungle-like tangle within its prescribed confines, although a certain wildness of habit does become most. Let me also just say here that kiwis take a very long season to ripen – anywhere from 150 to almost 300 days depending on cultivar; so in our cooler zones, frost may thwart your efforts, and, as most are male or female types, you will need one of each to culture kiwis successfully. That said, once established, they are exceptionally hardy, uncomplaining brutes, and eaten off the vine, as I'm not sure I've ever heard of anyone cooking a kiwi, any will add both color and health to your table.

Lavender

Lavandula angustifolia, L. stoechas

*"Then took Mary a pound of ointment of spikenard,
very costly; and anointed the feet of Jesus, and
wiped his feet with her hair; and the house was filled
with the odor of the ointment."*

–John 12:3

Fragrant lavender is indigenous to the mountainous regions of the western Mediterranean and has been employed there for millennia, mainly in a cleansing and aromatherapeutic vein. *Lavender* is thought to derive from either the Latin *lavare,* "to wash," or *livendulo,* "livid" or "bluish," in reference to the blossom color. According to W. T. Fernie, the Greeks called it *nardus,* after the town of Naarda in Syria, where they believed it originated, and it was broadly identified as "spikenard," this term marrying *nardus* with the plant's flower "spike."

In typical early herbal duality and countless other applications aside, lavender was prized both for its calming and aphrodisiacal effects, having been broadly employed to dispel headaches while, at the same time, being strewn about Cleopatra's chambers to entice both Julius Caesar and Mark Antony, and the well-known 1680 English rhyme "Lavender blue, dilly dilly . . ." originally containing the not-so-well-known lyrics, "Whilst you and I, diddle, diddle . . ." In the first century A.D., Dioscorides recommended lavender for indigestion, headaches, and sore throats and, externally, for cleansing wounds, and Pliny the Elder for menstrual problems, upset stomachs, kidney disorders, and insect bites. At the turn of the fifteenth century, "Charles the Mad" of France, who famously roamed his palaces howling like a wolf and was, at times, convinced that he was made of glass, had his seat cushions stuffed with "spikenard." John Parkinson recommended it in 1629 for ". . . bathes, ointment or other things that are used for cold cause . . . all griefes and paines of the head and brain . . . ," and, on a helpful household note, "to perfume linnen, apparell, gloves and leather . . ." Elizabeth I was known to use lavender to treat her migraines; by 1653 Nicholas Culpeper was lauding lavender for ". . . the tremblings and passions of the heart, and faintings and swounings . . ."; and by 1655, during the Great Plague of London, lavender was being hawked on every street corner as a prophylactic.

Modern medicine has confirmed lavender's effectiveness in treating stress and headaches, the British herbalist Maude Grieve advising in 1931 that "a tea brewed from Lavender tops, made in moderate strength, is excellent to relieve headache from fatigue and exhaustion, giving the same relief as the application of Lavender water to the temples." As well, lavender was broadly employed as

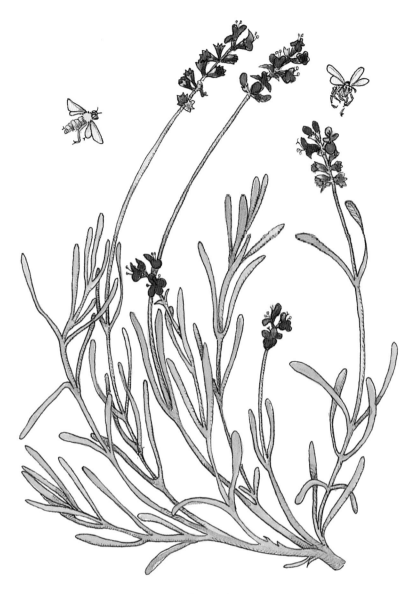

Lavender

a topical antiseptic for wounds and burns in the trenches of World War I, and, again according to Mrs. Grieve, "In France, it is a regular thing for most households to keep a bottle of Essence of Lavender as a domestic remedy against bruises, bites and trivial aches and pains, both external and internal."

There are a number of lavender types, the two main ones being "English lavender," *Lavendula angustifolia,* and "French lavender," *Lavendula stoechas,* the original Mediterranean "spikenard" of old, the principal differences being leaf form – the French variety having larger, more rounded leaves – and quality of fragrance – educated noses infinitely preferring the English types like the popular cultivars 'Hidcote' and 'Munstead'. A Mediterranean native, lavender will only truly prosper in a light, sandy soil in a dry, open, sunlit position. If you can achieve that, plant away in great, fragrant billows, and employ the fresh or dried flowers in everything from teas and cordials to linen rinses, bath soaks, sachets, and potpourris. Or why not just hang a big, beautiful bundle of wands from an accommodating rafter and allow it to scent your precincts?

Leek

Allium porrum

"Next to the Lion and the Unicorn,
The Leeke the fairest emblyn that is worne."
—Harleian MS., *A Collection of Pedigrees,* fifteenth century

*L*eeks, as members of the ancient *Allium* family, were probably being consumed by our prehistoric ancestors long before man first put rudimentary hoe to ground. Most botanists agree that *Alliums,* actually members of the greater *Liliacceae,* or lily, family, have been under domestic cultivation for at least 5,000 years and being storable, transportable, and easily grown in a broad spectrum of soils and climates, probably constitute one of the world's earliest food crops. In Numbers 11:5 of the Bible, the leek and its cousins onion and garlic are among the food plants pined for by the children of Israel following their great exodus: "We remember the fish, which we did eat in Egypt freely, the cucumbers and the melons and the leeks and the onions and the garlic."

In India, however, an ordinance of the sixth century B.C. proclaimed that leeks were prohibited from being consumed by the "twice born," and were fit only for the lower orders. In the first century A.D., the Emperor Nero ate leeks cooked in oil to clear his voice for singing, and for this hopeful habit he was derisively called Porrophagus, or "leek-eater.' In that same century, the Romans introduced leeks into England and Wales, and by the twelfth century, the leek had become the Welsh national symbol, worn in one's hat on St. David's Day in remembrance of King Cadwallader, who, in the seventh century, induced the Britons to wear leeks on their helmets to distinguish them from the Saxons in battle. Wales's association with leeks was also recorded by William Shakespeare in *Henry V,* when the Welsh Captain Fluellen reports to young King Hal, ". . . the Welshmen did good service in a garden where leeks did grow, wearing leeks in their Monmouth caps; which, your majesty know, to this hour is an honourable badge of service . . ."

Additionally, leeks were valued for their herbal benefits, an Old English adage cautioning one to "eat leeks in Lide [March] and ramsins [wild garlic] in May and all the years after physicians may play." Modern medicants confirm that leeks, like their cousins onion and garlic, are impressively good for you with high concentrations of flavonoids and antioxidant polyphenols as well as healthy doses of vitamin K.

There are many handsome varieties of leek going by such evocative names as 'Blue Solaise', 'King Richard', 'American Flag', and 'Dawn Giant', all boasting snowy bulbs, thick, succulent shafts, and that signature cockade of elegantly arching blue leaves. Leeks are also exceptionally carefree in the garden, as, like other members of the Allium family, they seem to come with their own built-in pest resistance as well as being extremely cold hardy; I've been known to pull these garden stalwarts out of the snow in March. They do, however, have quite a long growing season, usually 100 to 120 days, so start them in a seed tray indoors 6 to 8 weeks before last frost, then plant out in early spring by dibbling holes about 6 inches apart and dropping a young leek into each, then watering but not filling with soil, which will allow each leek sufficient space to enlarge.

Historically, the French were known to call leeks the "asparagus of the poor" until, as the story goes, sometime after 1910, when he became chef de cuisine at Manhattan's Ritz-Carlton Hotel, chef Louis Diat created the soup he famously named for his home-town of Vichy. Therefore, I urge you all to whirl up some potatoes and leeks softened in chicken broth with a portion of cream, then cool, adjust seasonings, sprinkle with chives, and have at a classic vichyssoise.

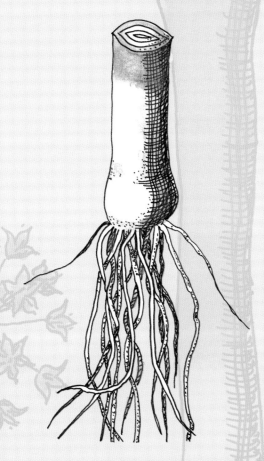
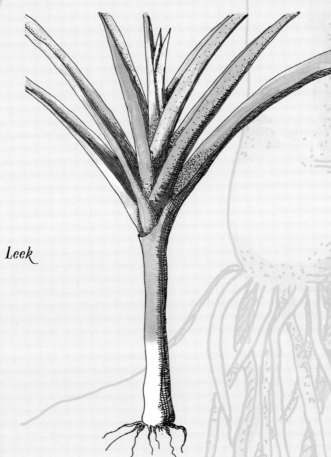

Leek

Lemon

Citrus limon

" . . . you spill a universe of gold
a yellow goblet of miracles
a fragrant nipple of the Earth's breast . . ."

—Pablo Neruda, "Ode to a Lemon," 2005

Certainly the lemon is originally native to the Far and/or Middle East, with various claques championing Malaysia, Myanmar, China, and India as its birthplace. A "lemon-shaped" earring found in Malaysia, dating to 2500 B.C., has made Malaysia the site du jour, but that shape could also accurately describe the citron and the lime, so the debate rages on. Additionally, some, like the Israeli historian Samuel Tolkowsky, believe lemons were known in Italy as early as A.D. 300, as a mosaic floor dating to second-century Carthage displays recognizable lemons, while others identify the Carthaginian image as a citron and have the lemon entering Italy in the eleventh century

94

with the returning Crusaders. As all citrus were also essentially lumped together histor-ically, this clearly remains a huge gray (if tartly flavored) area. What seems beyond debate is that by the end of the fifteenth century, the infamous Cesare Borgia was sending gifts of lemons and oranges to his wife in France, John Gerard notes both "limons" and "orenges" in use in England in his *Herball* of 1636, and, by the end of the seventeenth century, Louis XIV was bestowing tokens of oranges and lemons upon his royal favorites, who apparently employed them to "redden their lips."

The lemon was introduced to the New World by Christopher Columbus in 1493, and by the mid-sixteenth century, the Spanish missionary Bartolomé de las Casas noted them growing in the West Indies. Most botanists place introduction into North America via Florida at some moment between 1513, when Ponce de León arrived in search of his fountain of youth, and 1565, when St. Augustine, the first Floridian colony, was established.

Medicinally, like all citrus, lemons are excellent sources of both vitamin C and anti-oxidant and anticarcinogenic phytonutrients.

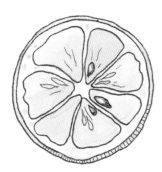

As you have probably suspected, the lemon is native to our warmest climates and, therefore, will be hardy to USDA zones 8b to 10 alone, which will make perennial culture decidedly difficult for most of you. Therefore, while there are excellent stan-dard lemon cultivars like 'Eureka', 'Lisbon', and 'Ponderosa' available as trees to those of you in those climates that will support them, here I will turn your attention to the dwarf, eminently pot-cultivable Lemon 'Meyer' (Improved). Known in China since the fourteenth century and thought to be a cross between a lemon and a mandarin orange, the first 'Meyer' in the U.S. was carried into California from Beijing in 1908 by Frank N. Meyer, a U.S. government botanist, and subsequently named for him. Unfortunately, this original 'Meyer' was prone to the Citrus tristeza virus until it was "improved" in the mid-1950s by Don Dillon, Sr., of White Winds Growers in Fremont, California, when he discovered a virus-free clone in their test fields. All lemon 'Meyer' Improved plants derive to this day from that single "improved" mother tree.

All lemon trees are lovely, with their glossy green leaves and intensely fragrant white flowers, most growing to 10 to 12 feet, but the 'Meyer' may be kept to 8 feet or under, depending on your pruning preferences and the size of your pot, and is also self-fruitful, admirably unfinicky, and notoriously prolific, often flowering twice a year. However, it's the Meyer's ruddy golden fruits that are the real treasure, notable for their unique lemon/orange taste, juicy amplitude, and thick, admirably candy-able and zest-able rind. Just give your 'Meyer' a healthy dose of sun and water, indoors and out, roll indoors when temperatures hit below 30 degrees, rotate occasionally, and you will be rewarded all year long on all kinds of matchless sensory levels.

Lemon Balm

Melissa officinalis

"The several chairs of order look you scour
With juice of balm and every precious flower."
−William Shakespeare, *Merry Wives of Windsor,* 1600

*I*n this tome, I will introduce you to a number of notable lemon-scented herbal presences in the garden, but none so stalwartly age-old and hardy-habited as lemon balm, a *Lamiaceae* (mint) family member native to southern Europe and the Mediterranean. Known simply as "balm" antiquely – an abbreviation of "balsam," which originates from the Hebrew *bal smin,* meaning "chief of sweet-smelling oils" – lemon balm is not the pined-for "balm in Gilead" referenced in the Bible, which is the true balsam of Judea. However, lemon balm soon managed to acquire both that legendary plant's herbal mantle and its title. *Melissa* derives from the Greek for "honeybee" (*mel* = "honey"), and Pliny the Elder says of bees and lemon balm, "When they are strayed away, they do find their way home by it."

At the turn of the sixteenth century, the Swiss physician Paracelsus designated a decoction of lemon balm his "elixir vitae," William Rhind commenting in 1865, ". . . whereby he was to renovate man; and, if he did not bestow upon him absolute immortality, to produce a very close approximation to that state." The London Dispensary endorsed the same view in 1696, affirming that an infusion of lemon balm ". . . given every morning, will renew youth, strengthen the brain and relieve languishing nature," and John Evelyn described it in 1699 as ". . . strengthening the memory, and powerfully chasing away melancholy." According to Maude Grieve, lemon-balm tea was famously imbibed by both Llywelyn, thirteenth-century prince of Glamorgan, who lived to be 108 years old, and one John Hussey of Sydenham, who lived to be 116. In 1865, however, William Rhind cuts sharply to the herbal chase in reference to the elixir vitae of Paracelsus: "Such strange conceits of ill-directed minds have . . . long gone

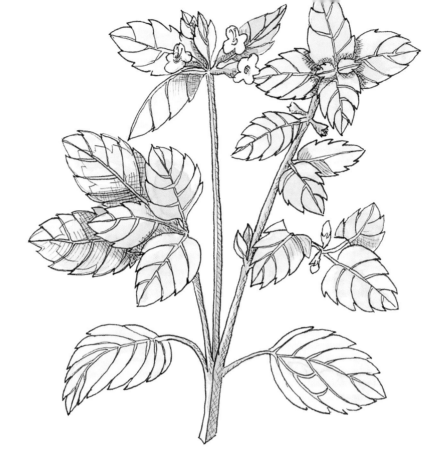

Lemon Balm 'All Gold'

by; and balm, stripped of its fancied virtues, is now only employed as an infusion in preparing a cooling drink, or in giving flavor to a weak, factitious wine."

Externally, lemon balm has had far more enduring support, as Pliny the Elder reports in the first century A.D., "It is of so great virtue that though it be but tied to his sword that hath given the wound it stauncheth the blood," with Gerard concurring, "the juice of Balm glueth together greene wounds." In fact, lemon balm's balsamic oils make it an excellent surgical dressing – these oils not only are anti-putrescent but also actually starve wounds of oxygen as their balsamic resins seal them from infection. And, frankly, whatever Rhind's opinion, lemon balm tea is still a mighty soothing thing.

Lemon balm is clearly identifiable as a mint clan member, with square, branching stems to 2 feet, oval- to heart-shaped, jagged-edged leaves, and small white or yellowish flowers. There is the general-issue green variety and also a variegated ('Variegata') variety, which, however, is prone to reverting to green in the heat of most of our summers, as well as the radiant 'All Gold' or 'Aurea' type, boasting chartreuse leaves and constituting a perfect plant to sparkle up a semi-shady corner of your vegetable or herb plot, although it will do just as well in full sun. Perennially hardy to USDA zone 4, lemon balm, being a mint, will pretty much survive anywhere, and will spread with some rapaciousness, so a bit of curtailment will be of the essence. Cut back frequently in season to prevent flowering and seeding, and entirely in fall, and, just like mint, your stand will re-sprout winningly in spring.

This is definitely a tea idea: hot or cold, comforting or refreshing – take your pick.

Lemon Verbena

Aloysia triphylla

*Keep an infusion of lemon verbena in a spray
bottle in the refrigerator and give
your face a spritz at the first sign of the blahs.*

I had always imagined that lemon verbena (or verveine), with its remarkable citrusy scent, must have a long and distinguished herbal and culinary history. For one thing, *verbena* was the catchall early Roman term for "sacred herb," and the vervaine of European legend was believed to have been used to stanch the wounds of the

Savior on Golgotha Hill. In medieval times, amulets of verbena root were habitually worn about the neck to ward off pestilence and witchcraft, and verbena leaves and flowers were employed in countless incantations, evil-dispelling ointments, and erstwhile love potions by aspiring sorcerers.

So imagine my surprise when I learned that these near-miraculous achievements belong to another plant and family entirely, vervaine, or *Verbena officinalis*, and that lemon verbena *(Aloysia triphylla),* or verveine is actually a South American plant native to Argentina, Chile, and Peru, and was not introduced into Europe until the late eighteenth century, when it was imported to Spain for the manufacture of perfume. Why it was named both "lemon verbena" and verveine (vs. vervaine), when it not only doesn't remotely resemble but also isn't remotely related to *Verbena officinalis,* is a point absolutely no one seems to be able to answer to my satisfaction. We do know, however, that *Aloysia* derives from Maria Louisa – princess of Parma and wife of King Charles IV of Spain, into which country the herb was first delivered – and *triphylla,* from this plant's immensely fragrant whorls of three (*tri*) leaves (*phylla*). This is not to say, however, that lemon verbena did not achieve its own medicinal and culinary reputation once it reached the continent. It was widely touted during the nineteenth and early twentieth centuries as an antispasmodic, carminative, sedative, antimicrobial, digestive aid, and fever reducer. Today, lemon verbena is one of the reigning darlings of aromatherapy, as its leaves stay fragrant nearly everlastingly, and teas and infusions of the leaves have a broadly "soothing" reputation, lemon verbena's volatile oils and flavonoids being calming to both the stomach and the nerves, helping to reduce fever, and, applied as a skin tonic, serving as a refreshing antibacterial for conditions like acne and boils.

As you might expect, being a South American native, lemon verbena is perennially hardy only to USDA zone 8, but it may easily be grown as an annual or alternatively employed as a potted plant and taken indoors for the winter, although it is somewhat prone to white fly and, being deciduous, may thank you for your trouble by dropping its leaves. Better to purchase a plant each spring and watch it grow into a lovely, willowy thing with slender, lanceolate, highly lemon-scented leaves and tiny pale lavender-to-white flowers in the summer, and growing to 3 feet in a single season. Lemon verbena loves sun and warmth, and in zones that don't veer below 27 degrees, you may cut the plant back rather brutally and mulch the crown well, and it should resprout easily in spring. Also, snipping back the growing tips occasionally in season will promote branching and keep your plant nicely dense and bushy.

When the leaves are young and tender, chop them into green or fruit salads; older leaves are perfect for an aromatic and immensely comforting cup of tea. Here, however, I will suggest the concoction of a flavorful and healthful *eau-de-vie:* chop ½ cup of fresh leaves, add to a jar with 4 cups of vodka, let stand for two weeks, add 2 cups of sugar, shake to dissolve, let stand for another two weeks, strain, and sip when your day has had too many hours.

Lemongrass

Cymbopogon citratus, C. flexuosus

*Contemporary spiritualists advise adding a sprinkling of
lemongrass to your tarot bag to "keep your cards attuned,"
as well as scattering lemongrass around the table before readings.*

Lemongrass, a native of India and Sri Lanka and cousin to vetiver *(Vetiveria ziza-nioides)*, citronella *(Cymbopogon nardus)*, and palmarosa *(Cymbopogon martini)* in the *Gramineae* family, is a fairly recent star in the global herbal firmament and is still best known for its lemony presence in Thai and Vietnamese cuisine as well as for the employment of its essential oil in perfumes. There are two basic varieties of lemongrass: the West Indian *(Cymbopogon citratus)* and East Indian *(Cymbopogon flexuosus)* types, the main difference being that the West Indian type alone contains the active analgesic compound myrcene.

Lemongrass has had a long history of herbal application in both India and Africa, where, known alternatively as "Fevergrass," it is traditionally employed in Ayurvedic medicine to combat Jwara, or "fever." *The Charaka Samhita,* the oldest extant Sanskrit medical treatise, which dates to the third century B.C., claimed that during the evolution of human ailments, fever was the first to come into being, and it was disturbing not only to the body but the mind and soul as well. In Tanzania and Kenya, an infusion of lemongrass was also taken historically for fevers as well as being employed as a body wash and perfume, and the Zulu were known to use the plant juice for ritual cleansing. Citral, the main chemical constituent of lemongrass's essential oil, is antiviral, antiseptic, and antibacterial, making it a splendid astringent for troublesome complexions, and recent research also suggests that lemongrass oil is highly effective as a sedative, acting on the central nervous system and, applied to the temples, being especially useful in headache and stress relief. The only caveat here is that essential lemongrass oil is a powerful thing and should be diluted before application.

Lemongrass

As you might suspect from its name, lemongrass is a tall, graceful, heavenly scented "fountain" of a grassy plant, boasting light green blades growing from 3 to 6 feet and offering both wonderful texture and movement in a bed or border, as well as constituting an elegant upright focal point at the center of a cascading potted planting. Clearly native to tropical climes, lemongrass prefers humidity and warmth and is hardy only to USDA zones 10 and 11, so the rest of us will just have to treat it as an annual or pot it up and drag it inside come winter. Lemongrass is easily propagated by crown division; or, if you can find some in the store, try peeling off the outer leaves of the store-bought stalks, standing them upright in a jar of water on a sunny windowsill until they root, and then planting them.

Culinarily, it is the pale tubular core, resembling a slim scallion bulb, inside the fibrous outer layers of a lemongrass stalk that is of interest here. To use, cut the stalk to about 6 inches, remove two layers, and then gently bruise it along its length using the side of a large knife or a rolling pin to encourage that citrusy aroma. Slivers of this tender core may then be added to pungent Thai and Vietnamese-style broths and stews, imparting a rich lemon savor, or may be brewed into a delicious fever- and stress-reducing tea.

However, due to the popular employment of this flavorful herb by the fragrance industry, let me direct you here to the concoction of a refreshing take on a very useful insect repellant: mix a teaspoonful of lemongrass oil with half as much eucalyptus oil and ¼ cup vegetable oil. Shake up in a glass bottle and dab on uncovered flesh as needed of a summer night.

Lettuce

Lactuca sativa

"He has sprouted; he has burgeoned;
He is lettuce planted by the water.
He is the one my womb loves best."

–Sumerian Song, 3000 B.C.

Lettuce is another ancient vegetable family that, while permuting into a thousand variations on a theme, has at the same time remained extremely close to its wild roots. A relative of chicory, the *Lactuca sativa* family is a descendant of the bitter wild lettuce (*Lactuca serriola*) native to Asia Minor and the trans-Caucasus. The milder, more refined var. *sativa* is believed to have originated in the Mediterranean region but has been found growing as far afield as Europe, Africa, and the Near East since recorded time. Both the common and Latin names of lettuce have their roots in the milky, mildly soporific juice it releases when cut or bruised; *lettuce* deriving from the French *laiteux*, meaning "milky," and *Lactuca*, coming from the Latin word for milk.

Historically, lettuces of the ancient world were divided into two camps: the cabbage-headed lettuces, which were of a round, relatively loose-leaved habit, and the "Cos," or "Romaine," lettuces, of a tighter, more conical and elongated profile. A famous wall fragment of the third millennium B.C., portraying Min, Egyptian God of fertility and bounty, shows him in full phallic salute by an offering of stylized but readily identifiable Romaines.

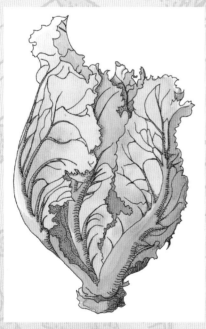

Lettuce 'Australian Yellowleaf'

Lettuce 'Lollo Rosso'

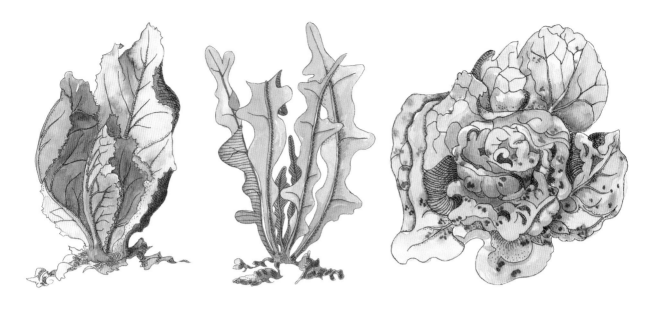

Lettuce 'Merlot'   Lettuce 'Royal Oakleaf'   Lettuce 'Forellenschluss'

The gastronomic and medicinal virtues of lettuce were being noted by the Greek historian Herodotus of Halicarnassus in 550 B.C., by Hippocrates, the Greek mathematician, in 430 B.C., by Aristotle in 356 B.C., and by Pliny the Elder, who described no fewer than nine types of lettuce under cultivation in the first century A.D. It was Columbus who introduced the *Lactuca sativa* family to the New World in 1494, and by the end of the seventeenth century, lettuce could be found growing in virtually every European colony in North America. This rapid popularity was due not only to lettuce's famously edible cooling crispness and short maturation time, but also to its wide usage as a medicinal plant, John Evelyn in his *Acetaria* of 1699 asserting that it ". . . allays Heat, bridles Choler, extinguishes Thirst, excites Appetite, kindly Nourishes, and above all represses Vapours, conciliates Sleep, mitigates Pain . . .," and then optimistically if mystifyingly adding, ". . . besides the effect it has upon the Morals, Temperance and Chastity."

We now know that lettuces, being about 95 percent water, are not thrillingly efficacious in terms of health benefits, but they're extremely low in calories and nicely high in fiber, vitamins K and A, plus a sprinkling of phytonutrients. Additionally, lettuces have existed in a startling and truly beautiful range of shadings, cuttings, and frilly curlings since very early in the recorded history of vegetables, and there is an almost infinite number of lettuces whose physical attributes are commendable. Some of our favorites on the farm are the bright chartreuse 'Australian Yellowleaf', the frilly, red-tipped 'Lollo Rosso', the deep red varieties 'Outredgeous' and 'Merlot', the evocatively named 'Royal Oakleaf', and the crimson-splotched Romaine 'Troutback', or 'Forellenschluss'. For full heads in about 50 to 60 days from seeding, thin any of these to about 8 inches apart; however, I also recommend purchasing cut-and-come-again mixes from your favorite seed house, which, when cast in the garden, will start producing a pretty array of cut-able greens in about 30 days. In general, lettuces go to seed quickly in hot weather, so do plant early and late in the season. There is nothing more tender or freshly delicious than lettuce from the garden and, as John Evelyn continues in his *Acetaria*, "Lettuce . . . ever was and still continues the principal foundation of the universal tribe of sallets; which is to cool and refresh . . . ," so I'll take mine fresh-picked and dressed simply with a good, lemony vinaigrette.

Lime

Citrus latifolia, C. aurantifolia

*Between 1795 and 1815, after it was discovered that scurvy
could be cured with liberal doses of lime juice, some
1.6 million gallons of it were consumed by British sailors, giving
birth to the alternate apellation "limey."*

*C*itrus plants are antiquely native to India, the Malay Archipelago, and the Far East (think 4000 B.C.), sweet oranges probably originating in India, trifoliate oranges and mandarins in China, and the tarter citrus types, including the lime, in Malaysia. However, some taxonomists feel that the prehistoric antecedent of the entire clan may be the Microcitrus, a tall, small-fruited rainforest tree native only to northeastern Australia, and so unbelievably ancient that it probably grew before the continents of Australia and Asia drifted apart. Recent molecular evidence unearthed by Chinese scientists confirmed that the lime's ancient forbearers were a species of *Papeda*, that citrus subgenus that includes the Kaffir lime, as its female ancestor, and the citron *(Citrus medica)* as its ancient male antecedent.

The lime made that familiar voyage into North Africa and Arabia along the spice roads, and was finally imported into the southern Mediterranean in the fourth century B.C., probably with the returning legions of Alexander the Great. From the second century B.C. onward, citrus groves of many descriptions were founded all over southern Europe, and by the fifteenth century A.D., potted specimens, which could be carted into glass houses, popularly dotted parterres across the continent. Columbus is credited with delivering the lime to Hispaniola in 1493, from whence it was carried to Florida by Spanish settlers at the turn of the sixteenth century. Medicinally, although not as much of a powerhouse as its cousin the lemon, the lime is still an excellent source of vitamin C and antioxidancy through its impressive collection of phytonutrients.

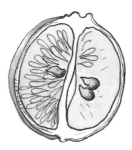

Ancient hybrid that it is, the lime has continued to interbreed with its relations, producing lime-esque progeny like the Kaffir lime *(Citrus hystrix),* a *Papeda* relative, the limequat *(lime × kumquat),* and the sweet lime *(Citrus limetta).* Here, however, we will concentrate on our most familiar lime, the Persian lime *(Citrus latifolia)* and, as in the case of the lemon, the one lime constituent most easily adaptable to pot culture,

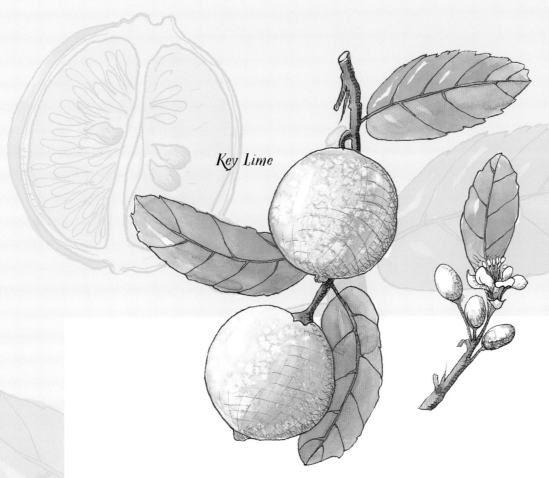

Key Lime

as, being a truly tropical type, the lime will not be hardy below USDA zones 9-10. The Persian lime, known only in cultivation, is most likely a cross between a Key lime *(Citrus aurantiifolia)* and a lemon *(Citrus × limon)* and, as you might hazard to guess, is most probably antiquely native to Persia, although it was first brought into culture in what is now southern Iraq.

As with all citrus, they are handsome trees with glossy leaves and wonderfully fragrant white blossoms, so, if you are in the right zone to culture one, I urge you to do so. However, for the rest of us, I will steer you to one of the Persian lime's ostensible parents, the Key lime *(Citrus aurantifolia)*. A semi-dwarf tree, the Key lime is both a rapid grower and easily prunable to your preferred habit, an added bonus being that it will produce heavily even when young. The fruit of the Key lime is much smaller than that of the Persian variety, nearly spherical, sweeter of savor, thinner of skin and, interestingly, is fully ripened when it turns from green to yellow. A Key lime cultured in a container will be blissfully happy out on your terrace in a nice sunny position when temperatures remain above 60 degrees, and will do splendidly indoors in a sunny spot in winter in the same temperature range.

Culinarily, there is nothing more refreshing than a cooling glass of home-made limeade of a sweltering afternoon, so squeeze a few into an icy pitcher, add sugar, and sip at your whim.

Lingonberry

Vaccinium vitis-idaea

*The lingonberry was so vital a food source in ancient Scandinavia
that, in Iceland, thirteenth-century law decreed that the
number of berries you could pick on land not your own was limited
to what you could consume on the spot.*

*T*he lingonberry, also known as the cowberry, fox berry, mountain cranberry, partridgeberry, and, of course, that catchall red "whortleberry," is a small evergreen shrub of the *Ericaceae* family that grows wild in the mountainous regions of Scandinavia, Russia, Canada, and, in the United States, Maine. Remains of lingonberry wine found in ancient Danish graves indicates human consumption as far back as 1500 B.C. during the Bronze Age, and lingonberries are as much a fruit staple in Scandinavia as their *Vaccinium* cousins blueberries and cranberries are in North America. A near ringer for the cranberry, lingonberries, with their bright red fruit and neat, small-scale leaves, are coveted not only for their sweeter taste but also for their exceedingly decorative habit. In fact, in 1651, André Mollet, French gardener to Sweden's Queen Christina, recommended in his *Le Jardin de Plaisir* that the lingonberry be employed for the edging of parterre gardens rather than the traditional box.

Lingonberry

It was the Italian Lorenzo Magalotti, editor of the *Saggi di Naturali Esperienze,* who wrote the first European account of the lingonberry in 1674, and the lingonberry figures heavily in Christian Gartner's *Hortikultura* of 1694, which recommended it for both culinary and herbal usage. Carl Linnaeus had identified the lingonberry by 1748, they were included by the Swedish economist Johan Fischerstrom in his dictionary of natural science of 1779, and Anders Retzius, the Swedish botanist and entomologist, wrote glowingly of them in his tome on economically useful plants of 1806. Aside from being, as noted, a strikingly ornamental plant, the lingonberry, according to Retzius, was excellent for fever patients, enjoyed historic employment as an anti-scorbutic and diarrhea medication, and tea brewed from the lingonberry's leaf was recommended for both rheumatism and urinary tract infections. Modern science has revealed that lingonberries are healthily loaded with vitamins B and C, beta-carotene, and other cancer-fighting anthocyanins, as well as potassium, calcium, magnesium, and phosphorus.

Yet with all these sterling attributes plus an iron constitution, being hardy in USDA zones 2 through 8, the lingonberry has, tragically, never really caught on outside its native habitat. This is a distinct loss for home gardeners, as the lingonberry is one of the prettiest ground cover ideas going: an ornamental triple threat of pretty flower, gorgeous fruit, and handsome leaf and habit, growing to a delightfully compact 8 to 10 inches. Planted in a mass, lingonberries, although conveniently self-fruitful, are spectacular as a thick carpet of finely wrought foliage, robust even in the bitterest cold, and dotted with pretty pink-blushed, bell-shaped white flowers in spring and sparkling vermillion fruit in fall.

As mentioned, lingonberry plants are rather difficult to find, so I will not recommend just one type here, although some of the most popular varieties are 'Sussi', the very first lingonberry to be selected and named; 'Regal', developed at the University of Wisconsin; 'Masovia', and 'Koralle'. All are hardy in the extreme, will prefer some shade in zones 6 to 8, and insist on soil on the acidic side (pH 3.5 to 5). Plants can be slow to establish and will require some attention to weeding, mulching, and watering during the first couple of seasons, so have a bit of patience.

Employ these fine berries, cooked and sweetened, exactly as you would a cranberry: in preserves, sauces for both desserts and meats, pie fillings, relishes, and so on, keeping in mind that lingonberry preserves as an accompaniment to Swedish meatballs and mashed potatoes is a treat you would be wise not to miss.

Lovage

Levisticum officinale

                            —Catherine Rogers, "Crone," 2005

*L*ovage, a brawny lug of a member of the *Apiaceae* family, looks like nothing so much as a stand of celery on steroids, although it is actually a cousin to anise, dill, caraway, cumin, and fennel. Native to the mountainous regions of the Mediterranean, southern Europe, and Asia Minor, and also known commonly as "Sea Parsley," "Love Herb," and the puzzlingly evocative "Love Rod," the Greeks called it *ligustikon* and the Romans *ligusticum,* as it apparently grew rampantly in ancient Liguria. The Latin *Ligusticum* was, for some reason, transmuted to *Levisticum,* then becoming *luvesche* in Old French, the heartrending *loveache* in Middle English, and, finally, our modern *lovage.*

Celtic legend held that if lovage was dug up on Good Friday under cover of night, it would ward off both witches and the devil, and Felix Wurtz, the sixteenth-century Swiss physician, maintained that "if lovage roots are dug while the sun is passing over the sign of Aries, and they are fastened around the neck, they will make the approved remedy for atrophy and decline of the limbs." Lovage was another of the useful food plants grown by Charlemagne in his imperial garden in the ninth century A.D.; Hildegard of Bingen, Sybil of the Rhine, recommended it for sore throat in the eleventh century; and in medieval and Renaissance Europe, lovage's roots, stalks, leaves, and seeds were all employed in treating digestive and respiratory ailments, rheumatism, bronchitis, and urinary tract infections. In 1653, Culpeper reports of lovage, "It opens, cures, and digests humours, and provokes women's courses and urine . . . takes away the redness and dimness of the eyes . . ." and ". . . removes spots and freckles from the face." In 1763, American herbalist John Sauer attributes these properties to lovage's ". . . warm, dry nature and . . . its numerous oily, volatile, alkaline salts." Our dear Mrs. Grieve, founder of The Whins Medicinal and Commercial Herb School in England, giving this typically brusque assessment in her *Modern Herbal* of 1931: "It is sometimes grown in gardens for its ornamental foliage, as well as for its pleasant odour, but it is not a striking enough plant to have claimed the attention of poets and painters, and no myths or legends are connected with it . . . ," although extremely reluctantly admitting "the roots and fruit [seeds] are aromatic and stimulant, and have diuretic and carminative action." Contemporary research concurs with lovage's soothing reputation as both an anti-allergen due to its quercetin content and an anti-inflammatory of the respiratory system due to its eucalyptol content, and a poultice of the fresh leaves applied to skin is efficacious in reducing the symptoms of psoriasis and acne.

Maude Grieve's lowly assessment aside, lovage is a striking perennial plant, hardy to USDA zone 4 and often growing to 6 feet tall, with hollow ribbed stalks similar to celery or angelica, glossy, toothed leaves, large umbels of greenish yellow flowers, and tiny oval seeds. Plant lovage in fertile soil in full sun with sufficient room to spread, cut back the flower stalks to encourage growth, and each spring should find this statuesque food plant hale and hearty. Most gourmets feel that lovage has a taste somewhere between celery and parsley, with roots, stems, leaves, and flowers all being edible.

Historically, lovage stalks were candied and consumed as a "sweet," and the young leaves are excellent in salads. However, I recommend the stalk and leaf tops as making the perfect aromatic bed and blanket for a roasted sea bass or salmon or such, imparting to it an excellent celery-esque green savor.

Marjoram

Origanum spp.

"The lily I condemned for thy hand,
And buds of marjoram had stol'n thy hair;
The roses fearfully on thorns did stand,
One blushing shame, another white despair . . ."

—William Shakespeare, Sonnet 99, 1609

*T*his is another clear case of herbal identity theft, as both marjoram and oregano, members of the genus *Origanum* in the greater *Lamiaceae*, or mint, family, have apparently masqueraded as one another since man was able to sit up and take nourishment. *Origanum* derives from the Greek *oros*, "mountain," and *ganos*, "joy," and, therefore, enchantingly translates to "joy of the mountain," upon which chalky flanks these herbal siblings grow natively through various parts of the Mediterranean and Eurasia.

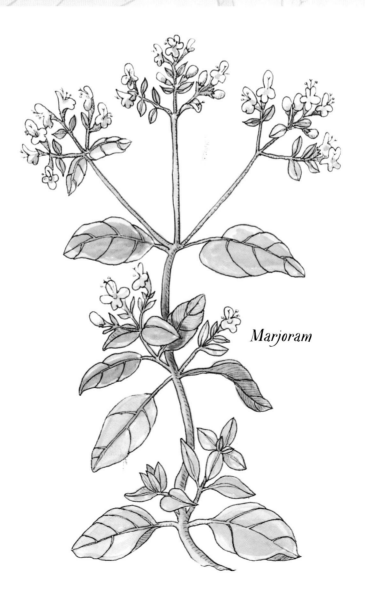

Marjoram

In truth, while marjoram is an "oregano," oregano is not a "marjoram," although it has been regularly and historically regarded as such. To wit, a sampling of this mind-boggling herbal bog: botanically, culinary oregano, also known as "wild marjoram," is *O. vulgare*, and marjoram (sometimes "sweet marjoram") is *O. majorana,* although, of course, 'Golden' marjoram, is botanically *O. vulgare*. Other constituents in this perplexing family include "pot" marjoram *(O. onites),* also called "Italian" or "Cretan" oregano, and "Greek" oregano *(O. vulgare hirtum),* the culinary champ of the family, also called "winter marjoram." Is everyone perfectly clear?

The ancient Greeks popularly planted "marjoram" on the graves of their dear deceased to ensure eternal peace, apparently incanting, "May many flowers grow on this newiy built tomb: not the dried up Bramble, or the red flower loved by goats; but Violets and Marjoram . . . ," and herbally, the Greeks made extensive use of "marjoram" both internally and externally for wounds, poisonings, convulsions, and dropsy, and were even known to graze their cattle in fields of it, in the belief that it produced tastier meat. In 1629, John Parkinson, apothecary to James I, identifies "marjoram" as the Amaracus referenced by Theophrastus, Dioscorides, and Pliny, popularly employed in the wound-healing *unguentum Amaricinum,* also noting that "the sweete mari-eromes are not only much used to please the outward senses in nosegays, and in the windows of houses . . . but are also of much use in Physicke, both to comfort the outward members, or parts of the body, and the inward also . . ." We now know that it's marjoram's healthy doses of rosmarinic acid and flavonoids that add up to truly admirable antioxidancy, its saponins provide exceptional healing properties when a poultice of leaves is applied to external cuts and abrasions, and an infusion of marjoram is an excellent general tonic, helping to relieve anxiety, headaches, coughs, cramps, and stomach upsets.

As discussed, there are a good number of "marjorams" from which to choose, the most visible being the familiar "sweet marjoram" *(O. marjorana),* but there are very pretty gold and gold-tipped varieties (*O. vulgare* 'Aureum' and *O. vulgare* 'Gold-Tipped', respectively) as well as compact *(O. vulgare compactum),* dwarf (*O. vulgare* 'Nanum'), and "pot" *(O. onites)* types. If I were going to plant one variety, I would head right to the ''Aureum' cultivar, with its brilliant chartreuse leaves and marvelous ground-cover habit, making it a very sunny statement in the herb garden indeed. Most marjorams are only hardy to USDA zone 7, although they occasionally overwinter here at the farm in 6b, so those of you in cooler zones will have to treat them as annuals. You can either sow indoors six weeks before last frost or, if you have a plant, marjoram propagates well from both cuttings and root division. All types will cherish a sunny spot in a good, loamy soil.

Culinarily, let me leave you here with a vision of a plump hen rubbed with garlic, salt, pepper, lemon, and marjoram, and then popped into a toasty oven.

Melon 'Queen Anne's Pocket'

Melon

Cucumis melo

"He who fills his stomach with melons is like he who fills it with light – there is a blessing in them."

—Middle Eastern proverb

*T*here is still some lingering debate over the exact origins of the melon, various claques championing such arid and diverse locales as Persia, Afghanistan, Africa, and Armenia. Ancient texts tell us that melons were cultivated in Babylonia in 2000 B.C. and that the Babylonian king Gilgamesh, hero of the epic Sumerian poem, was fond of them, and melon seeds discovered at Nuragic sites in Sardinia indicate that melons were delivered into Europe as early as the Bronze Age. The Assyrian king Merodach-Baladan was known to grow them in his gardens in the seventh century B.C., and when Moses led the Hebrew people into the desert, where they were destined to wander for a rather trying forty years, one of the foods they craved was melons, Numbers 11:5 reporting that they longed for "the fish, which we did eat in Egypt freely; the cucumbers, and the melons." By the seventh century A.D., watermelons were being cultivated in India and by the tenth century had been imported into China. Melons entered the Mediterranean region in the last century B.C. with the Moors bound for Andalusia, a wall painting depicting melons and dating to around the birth of Christ having been unearthed from the ruins of Herculaneum, and by the second century A.D., Galen, the Greek physician and herbalist, was debating the medicinal benefits of melons.

Melons were introduced into the New World by way of Haiti in 1494 on Columbus's second voyage, and by the seventeenth century, melons were under extravagant

Melon 'Prescott Fond Blanc'

cultivation in both France and Italy, the French calling them "Sucrin," for their sweetness, and Jean de la Quintinie, gardener to Louis XIV, planting seven varieties in the potager du Roi at Versailles. Oddly, there is scant evidence of medicinal employment across most of these cultures and it seems melons have always been mainly prized for their culinary appeal. However, modern medicine reveals melons, in general, are extremely low in calories, have almost zero fat, and provide healthy doses of vitamins A and C plus potassium and, with the orange and red-fleshed varieties, a good dollop of the anticarcinogen beta-carotene.

There are countless wonderful types of melons in all kinds of sizes, hues, and savors coming to us from all warm corners of the globe, from our familiar Cantaloupe, Honeydew, Crenshaw, and Watermelon to the far more arcane Golden Langkawi, Queen Anne's Pocket, and Prescott Fond Blanc. Therefore, it will be difficult to recommend just a few that will suit you and your growing environment; however, let me make a rather obvious point here: as fruits go, melons are on the largish size — not only in their girth and heft but in their decidedly rambunctious habit as well; "vigorous" would be an understatement. Therefore, all melons, will need plenty of space as well as a long, heat-filled season and even watering, but they grow easily from seed and all will reward you with striking fruit, deeply cut green leaves, and pretty yellow blossoms.

In the North, we start melons indoors a month prior to planting out when soil temperatures hit 70 degrees, and some gardeners rely on black plastic ground cover and row covers to boost the heat quotient. In humidity, various tiresome funguses and mildews might visit you on your voyage to ripeness, but all are controllable so don't be dissuaded. You should be harvesting the earliest of any of these sweet, brawny beauties in about 70 to 80 days.

For any type you might culture, my advice is to cut yourself a lavish wedge, sprinkle on a bit of lemon juice, and grab a spoon.

Melon 'D'Alger'

Watermelon 'Moon & Stars'

Peppermint

Mint

Mentha piperita, M. spicata, M. suaveolens

"In strewing of these herbs . . . with bounteous hands and free,
The healthful balm and mint from their full laps do fly."

–Michael Drayton, "Poly-Olbion," 1621

*T*he extensive mint brood is a genus of about 25 species and 600 varieties in the greater *Lamiaceae* clan, mainly indigenous to the Mediterranean, North Africa, and western Asia, with 7 types occurring natively in Australia and 1 in North America. Greek myth famously narrates the naming of this fresh-scented family in the tale of Pluto, sovereign of the Underworld, who falls for the nymph Menthe, raising the ire of his wife, Persephone, who tries to trample her, thus inspiring Pluto to transform Menthe into a shrubby plant with a wonderfully stimulating fragrance so that he would be reminded of her comely nature each time he trod her underfoot (just like a man . . .).

Peppermint, in particular, is broadly billed as the world's oldest medicine, with archeological evidence placing its initial application as far back as 8000 B.C., and biblically, mint appears as one of the herbal tithes of the Pharisees in Matthew 23:23: "Woe unto you, scribes and Pharisees, hypocrites! For ye pay tithe of mint and anise and cummin, and have omitted the weightier matters of the law, judgment, mercy, and faith . . ." Mint having been an ancient symbol of hospitality, the great Roman elegiac poet Ovid wrote in the first century A.D. of Baucis and Philemon scouring their serving board with mint before feeding the gods, and mint was also popularly strewn on temple and banquet hall floors to freshen the air. Pliny the Elder reported further in the first century A.D. that "…the very smell of it alone recovers and refreshes the spirits, as the taste stirs up the appetite for meat, which is the reason that it is so general in our acid sauces . . .," and Nicholas Culpeper recommended mint for nearly 40 ailments in 1653, for which he deemed it "singularly good." However, mint's most notable and enduring employments were basically twofold: as an infusion, as Parkinson relates, " . . to strengthen and comfort weak stomackes," and as an aromatherapeutic oil to relieve migraines, neuralgia, and rheumatic and muscular aches, Culpeper declaring, "Applied to the forehead and temples, it eases pains in the head . . ." Scientists have confirmed that mint's volatile oils and its impressive battery of flavonoids, phenolic acids, and triterpenes make it impressively antibacterial, antiviral, antifungal, anti-septic, carminative, and tonic.

As noted, there are many varieties of mint, from those truly ancient friends Peppermint *(Mentha piperita)*, Spearmint *(Mentha spicata)*, and Apple, or "Wooly," mint *(Mentha suaveolens)* to a host of relatively recent flavored hybrids like Chocolate mint (*Mentha piperita* 'Chocolate'), Lavender mint (*Mentha piperita* 'Lavendula'), and Pineapple mint plants (*Mentha suaveolens* 'Variegata'). All will provide you with handsome bushy plants, intensely fragrant leaves, and pretty flower wands ranging from white to purple. As anyone who has grown mint knows, once established, it can become a true invasive nuisance, sending out battalions of iron-tough runners, so it is always an excellent idea to surround your planting with a 10-inch-deep barrier of something non-biodegradable or head towards pot culture. Sun or partial shade and a rich soil is all mint will need to thrive and prosper, but do keep different types well separated, as they are prone to cross-pollination.

In deference to both Pliny and my esteemed parent, I would be remiss if I did not share my father's recipe for a mint sauce to accompany roast lamb: boil ½ cup of white vinegar with ¼ cup sugar until dissolved, pour over ½ cup of finely chopped mint, let stand for an hour, and ladle over a nice pink slice.

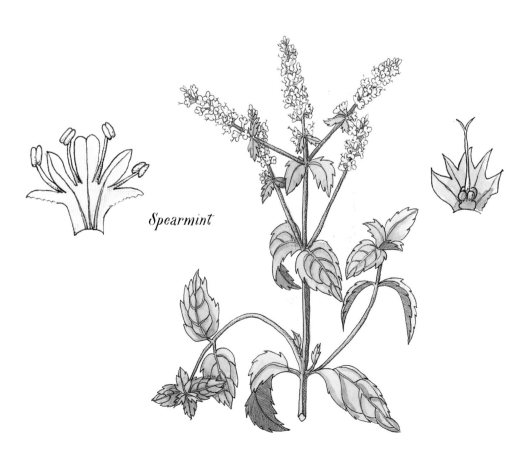

Spearmint

Mulberry

Morus rubra, M. nigra, M. alba

"Here we go round the mulberry bush,
On a cold and frosty morning."

—English nursery rhyme, eighteenth century

*F*ascinatingly, this familiar nursery rhyme was first sung by the inmates of the Wakefield House of Correction in England as they exercised around a mulberry tree in the prison grounds, and originated from some moment between 1786 and 1800. There are three basic types of mulberry: the white mulberry, *Morus alba,* native to China; the black mulberry, *Morus nigra,* anciently native to Iran and Mesopotamia; and the red mulberry, *Morus rubra,* native to the eastern United States, all being extremely antique to their natural habitats.

In China, legend holds that it was the empress Si Ling Chi who discovered silk 5,000 years ago when, while sipping tea in the palace garden, a cocoon fell into her cup from a white mulberry tree and, as she watched, a slim white thread unraveled itself. There are multiple references to the black mulberry in the Bible, 2 Samuel 5:24 reporting aggressively: "And let it be, when thou hearest the sound of a going in the tops of the mulberry trees, that then thou shalt bestir thyself, for then shall the Lord go out before thee, to smite the host of the Philistines." We also find mention of the mulberry in Ovid's telling of the sad tale of Pyramus and Thisbe, who, Romeo and Juliet-like, suicided in a mulberry's shade, the fruit, famously, being turned from white to black by their blood. The black mulberry was probably introduced into northern Europe and England by the Romans, and the most ancient black mulberry in Great Britain is said to be one at Syon House in Brentford dating to 1548.

Black Mulberry

The red mulberry has certainly grown in North America for millennia, and the Cherokees, Comanches, Seminoles, and Choctaws all consumed red mulberries whole, juiced, dried, and baked, and wove cloaks and made baskets from their fibrous inner bark and young shoots. As well, the Cherokee Nation employed an infusion of its bark as a purgative and laxative. Contemporary sources confirm all mulberries contain healthy doses of vitamins C, K, and A, plus a good dose of minerals and phytonutrients, and it's the red and black-fruited ones, due to their bulked-up load of anthocyanins, that really pour on the good-for-you juice.

All three mulberry species are very attractive trees, ranging in height from about 30 to 80 feet, although, oddly, the white mulberry is named for the color of its buds rather than its fruit, which can be white, lavender or black, while the red and black types are identified by fruit color. Mulberries are either dioecious or monoecious, although some cunning cultivars will change from one sex to the other and some will set fruit without any pollination — best to check these particulars with your local nursery. Additionally, all mulberries are both fairly unfinicky about soil quality and are drought tolerant, although all will prefer full sun and adequate spacing. They vary in cold tolerance by both species and cultivar, but, generally, the white mulberry is the cold-hardiest, followed by the red, with the black mulberry being hardy only to USDA zone 7, although the pretty 'Black Dwarf Weeping' variety is impressively hardy to zone 3. Mulberries of any color mainly resemble a large blackberry and can be so tasty, the great American reformer Henry Ward Beecher stated in 1846, that "I had rather have one tree of . . . mulberries than a bed of strawberries."

From any of these luscious beauties, why not concoct a rich sauce to accompany a roast fowl? To 2 cups crushed mulberries, add ½ cup brown sugar and a teaspoon each of cloves and allspice, bring to a boil, simmer until thick, sieve, and serve.

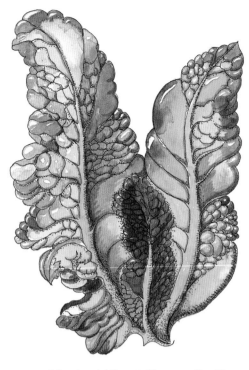

Mustard 'Giant Chinese Red'

Mustard

Brassica (Sinapsis) spp.

*"Sympathy without relief
Is like to mustard without beef."*
–Attributed to Samuel Butler, *Hudibras* (1663–1678)

There are about forty known mustard members of the Brassica family, cultivated either for their fiery seeds or their equally pungent greens. In the grown-for-seed category, the most commonly cultivated forms are White mustard (*B. hirta* syn. *Sinapsis alba*), Indian or Brown mustard (*B. juncea*), and Black mustard (*B. nigra*), differentiated mainly by the color of their seeds, white mustard being native to the Mediterranean, the Middle East, and North Africa, brown mustard to Asia and the foothills of the Himalayas, and black mustard to Africa, India, and Europe. The types grown for their edible tops are all *B. juncea* (var. *Chinensis*) and have grown wild in the Far East probably since the dawn of vegetation, although it seems most of the world remained resolutely unimpressed by them until recently.

Mustard derives from the Latin *mustum ardens,* "fiery wine," in reference to the ancient Sumerian custom of mixing mustard's peppery ground seeds with must, newly fermented grape juice. *Sinapsis,* this herbal plant's alternate botanical name, originates in the Greek *sinapi,* "that which bothers the eyes," for what I am assuming are obvious reasons. In two antique examples of remarkably wishful thinking, the early Danes believed a sizzling potion of mustard, ginger, and spearmint would cure a woman's frigidity, and German brides historically sewed mustard seeds into the hems of their wedding dresses to assure dominance in their households. By 1382, Phillip the Bold of Burgundy was so fond of mustard's famous condiment that he granted the armorial motto *moult me tarde,* "I wish for ardently," to the town of Dijon, France, and, by 1629 John Parkinson was commending it ". . . to serve as sauce both for fish and flesh . . . ," and also ". . . to warme and quicken . . . dull spirits . . ."

Contemporary herbalists still recommend mustard to promote digestion and as a plaster to relieve the pain of arthritis, rheumatism, and muscle pain, and modern science confirms that the seeds are excellent sources of calcium, magnesium, phosphorous, potassium, and vitamin A, while the greens offer those same benefits plus healthy swats of vitamins K and C.

Seed-wise, brown mustard is the type typically employed in Dijon and German mustards as well as the fiery English and Chinese varieties of that globally esteemed condiment, while white mustard alone is used in the manufacture of that mild, bright yellow mustard so dear to ballparks. Seed mustard plants are, for the most part, half-hardy but prolifically self-seeding annuals, some seed types, like rapeseed *(B. napus),* growing with such profligacy that they brighten entire fields with their acid color on most any continent you can name. The edible greens cultivars can be possessed of a bewildering range of leaf shapes and growth habits, from the neatly spoon-like and winged to the unwinged, notched, feathered, and curled, and from the compact and cabbage-like to the monstrously loose and clumpy, with wide variations in the strength of their "bite" as well. In fact, the dividing line between a Chinese cabbage *(B. rapa)* and a Chinese mustard *(B. juncea)* is suspiciously vague, basically boiling down to if it's got some fire, it's a mustard.

If you have a vegetable plot, some of the most popular of those are mizuna, a good number of "chois," and the flamboyant 'Giant Chinese Red' variety. Sauté or braise those with a bit of oil and garlic or stock for a piquant side dish, and if you have cultured some seed types, harvest, soak the seeds in water until softened, food process with a bit of cold water, doctor at your whim with a dollop of vinegar, honey, or a fresh herb like tarragon, and slather away.

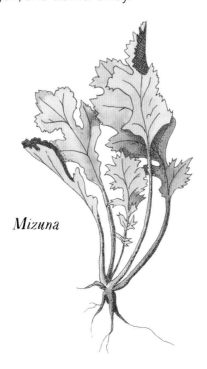

Mizuna

Nectarine

Prunus persica var. nectarina

*"The nectarine and curious peach
into my hands themselves do reach . . ."*
—Andrew Marvell, "The Garden," 1681

Contrary to popular opinion, the nectarine is not the wayward spawn of those promiscuous *Prunus* cousins the peach and the plum, but is simply a fuzzless peach spontaneously mutated in China, most probably around the first century B.C. Oddly, spontaneous mutation appears to be this fruit's most unique and enduring trait, as peach seeds may grow into nectarine trees, and vice versa, no less an authority than Charles Darwin having this to say in his *Variation of Animals and Plants Under Domestication* of 1868: "We have excellent evidence of peach-stones producing nectarine-trees, and of nectarine-stones producing peach-trees, of the same tree bearing peaches and nectarines . . ." I call it shameless. In fact, antiquely, there was absolutely no differentiation between the profligate pair, the eminent American pomologist U. P. Hedrick declaring in his *Peaches of New York* of 1917, "The established history of the nectarine goes back 2,000 years and then merges into that of the peach." The nineteenth-century French botanist Alphonse de Candolle reported that he "sought in vain for a proof that the nectarine existed in Italy in the time of ancient Rome," and it is Jacques Daléchamps, the French botanist, who finally gives the first reliable description of the nectarine in his *Historia generalis plantarum* of 1587, calling it *nucipersica,* or "Persian nut," because of its purported resemblance to the walnut.

The word *nectarine*, clearly derivative of *nectar,* seems to have been first coined by John Parkinson in his *Paradisi in Sole Paradisus Terrestris* of 1629, calling it " . . . more firme than the peach and more delectable in taste, and is therefore of more esteem, and that worthily." We find the first mention of the nectarine in America in historian Robert Beverly's *History and Present State of Virginia* of 1722, although some think that nectarines must have been delivered into California by the Spanish at a far earlier date.

Nectarines fall into two basic categories: yellow- and white-fleshed, the yellow-fleshed varieties being slightly more healthful, although, oddly, in comparison to other fruits, nectarines are not exceptionally high in anything, with indifferent amounts of vitamins A and C, niacin, dietary fiber, copper, and a slightly more impressive show of beta-carotene leading the fray. Still, they're certainly better for you than a kick in the teeth and mighty tasty.

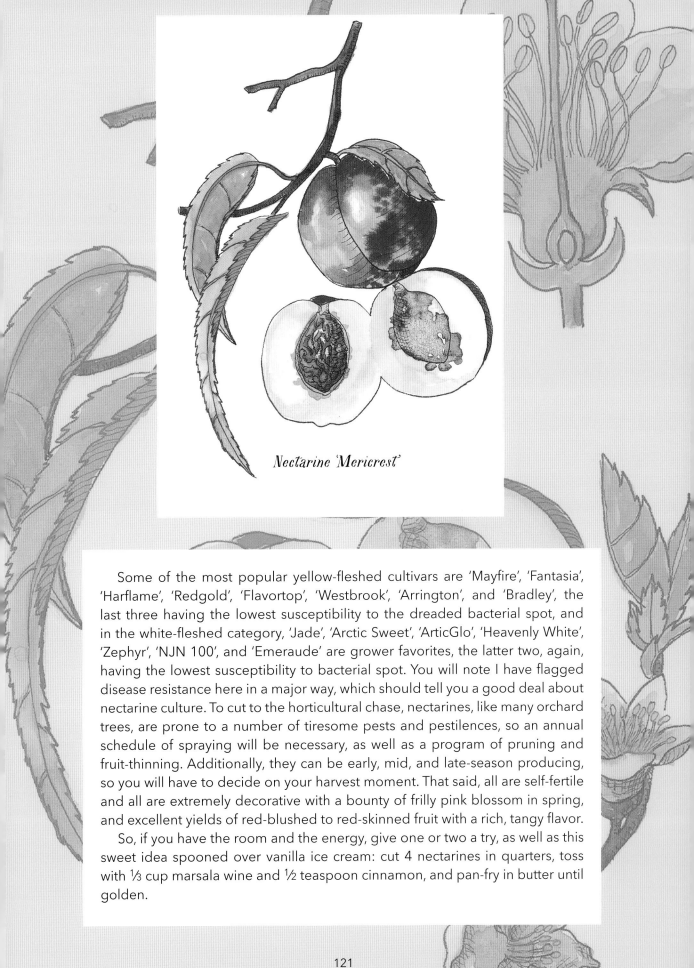

Nectarine 'Mericrest'

Some of the most popular yellow-fleshed cultivars are 'Mayfire', 'Fantasia', 'Harflame', 'Redgold', 'Flavortop', 'Westbrook', 'Arrington', and 'Bradley', the last three having the lowest susceptibility to the dreaded bacterial spot, and in the white-fleshed category, 'Jade', 'Arctic Sweet', 'ArticGlo', 'Heavenly White', 'Zephyr', 'NJN 100', and 'Emeraude' are grower favorites, the latter two, again, having the lowest susceptibility to bacterial spot. You will note I have flagged disease resistance here in a major way, which should tell you a good deal about nectarine culture. To cut to the horticultural chase, nectarines, like many orchard trees, are prone to a number of tiresome pests and pestilences, so an annual schedule of spraying will be necessary, as well as a program of pruning and fruit-thinning. Additionally, they can be early, mid, and late-season producing, so you will have to decide on your harvest moment. That said, all are self-fertile and all are extremely decorative with a bounty of frilly pink blossom in spring, and excellent yields of red-blushed to red-skinned fruit with a rich, tangy flavor.

So, if you have the room and the energy, give one or two a try, as well as this sweet idea spooned over vanilla ice cream: cut 4 nectarines in quarters, toss with ⅓ cup marsala wine and ½ teaspoon cinnamon, and pan-fry in butter until golden.

Okra

Abelmoschus esculentus

on the feeble stalks
ripe Okra swings steadily—
a farmer sings
—Adeleke Adeite, "Ripe Okra," 2013

A member of the *Mallow* family, making it a distant relation to cotton, the hibiscus, and the hollyhock, okra is believed to have originated in Ethiopia, and ancient varieties of this somewhat controversial food plant can still be found growing in the wild from Ethiopia to the White Nile in Egypt. Because of okra's linguistic absence in ancient Far East Indian, some botanists believe it found its way to India after the dawn of the Christian Era, wended its way into Arabia, and then was transported into Egypt by the invading Muslims around the seventh century A.D. Some of the earliest mentions of okra were made by the Spanish Moor Ibn Jubayr, who, traveling to Mecca in the years preceding the Third Crusade, saw it growing in Egypt sometime after A.D. 1183.

Okra is believed to have been introduced to the New World sometime before 1658 and most probably reached Brazil and Dutch Guiana with slaves from the Gold Coast of Africa. The okra delivered to the New World by slaves from Angola was natively called *ochinggombo,* which was later shortened to *ngombo*, then *gombo*, finally evolving into the familiar *gumbo*, a term which stood for both the native stew they enjoyed as well as the vegetable that still so famously thickens it. It is okra's acetylated acidic polysaccharide and galacturonic acid content, which is released when the pods are cut, that contributes to this thickening effect as well as to okra's rather mucilaginous reputation. In North America, okra was grown as far north as Philadelphia by 1748, and Thomas Jefferson noted it at Monticello in 1781. By about 1800, okra had become a plant staple of the American South, and several distinct varieties were under cultivation as early as 1806.

Okra 'Red Velvet'

Okra found medicinal employment across a host of early cultures it touched, the juice of the roots being used to treat cuts and wounds, the crushed leaves as an emollient poultice, and a decoction of the immature pods as a soothing digestive antispasmodic. Okra also wins accolades for being high in fiber and folate as well as vitamins C and K, and also contains good amounts of calcium and potassium.

Edible okra is actually the elegantly curved, edible seedpod of the okra plant: a notably tall, handsome garden presence, most varieties growing to about 4 feet and all boasting finely cut green leaves and large, truly beautiful hibiscus-like flowers with sunny, lemon-colored petals and deep ruby throats. Some of the most popular green varieties are 'Clemson Spineless', 'Perkins Mammoth', 'Jade', and 'Silver Queen', although there are many more, but my advice is to head towards one the gorgeous red-fruited, red-veined varieties like 'Red Velvet', 'Burgundy', 'Jing Orange', and 'Bowling Red', all of which will provide the additional luster of making a gorgeous crimson-colored statement in the garden.

Okra is one of those rare tropicals with a short growing season (a mere 60 days to harvest), so direct sow ½ to 1 inch deep when soil is well warmed up, then thin plants to 12 inches apart. Okra is really undeserving of its oft-maligned culinary possibilities, mainly the result of being harvested too late: pods should be picked when they are young and tender and only about 4 inches or so in length, about 4 to 5 days after flowering. The second mistake many cooks make is to overcook okra into slimy submission, as okra are natively crisp and fresh tasting. Why not do as they do down South and simply slice into bite-sized disks, dredge in cornmeal with a dash of salt and pepper, and fry briefly – you'll be surprised at the tasty result.

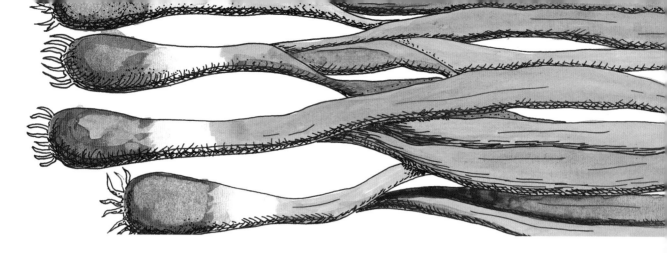

Bunching Onion 'Crimson Forest'

Onion

Allium cepa, A. fistulosum

"Onions make a man wink, drink and stink."
—Old English Proverb

*W*ild onions were undoubtedly consumed as far back as one can travel into our pre-history and are so ancient to so many parts of the globe that their origins are really completely obscure, although some believe them to be originally native to Asia or the Middle East. They were known to be under cultivation in Chinese gardens as early as the third millennium B.C., and a Sumerian inscription dating to 2400 B.C. relates, in an apparently kindly showing from the gods, "The oxen of the gods plowed the city governor's onion patches."

However, from all evidence, it was the Egyptians who were paranormally wild about the onion, seeing fit to stuff one into virtually every orifice a mummy offered, onions having been found adorning various pelvic and thoracic cavities, and in 1160 B.C. Ramses IV being entombed with onions filling his eye sockets. Many Egyptologists believe this interesting obsession was born of the ancient Egyptian view that the onion, with its circle-within-a-circle configuration, was a symbol of eternal life.

In the fifth century B.C., Hippocrates was prescribing onions as an efficacious healer of wounds, a sentiment echoed by Pliny the Elder in the first century A.D., and onions were so esteemed by Charlemagne in the eighth century that they were written into French feudal deeds. By the Middle Ages, the three main vegetable staples on any European table were beans, cabbages, and onions. Cultivated onions *(A. cepa)* found their way to the New World through Hispaniola (Haiti) with Christopher Columbus, although their wild cousins could already be found growing throughout North America.

Health-wise, onions are, in truth, about 85 percent water, and, while they contain fairly unimpressive quotients of vitamins and minerals, as suggested by Hippocrates and Pliny, they are a fine topical antiseptic and wound dressing as witnessed by their employment by Russian troops during World War II.

While there are hundreds of varieties of onions, both wild and cultivated, here, while mentioning *the A. fistulosum* types in passing, we will train the majority of our attention on the *Allium cepa* family, all of which were developed sometime in the 5,000-year-old history of onion selection and breeding. There are three main types: the yellow onion, with cultivars like 'Bermuda', 'Candy', 'Vidalia', and 'Walla Walla Sweet'; the white onion, with constituents like 'White Granex', 'White White', 'White Castle', and 'Sierra Blanca'; and the red onion, which numbers 'Red Wethersfield', 'Red Bull', 'Redwing', and 'Cabernet' in its ranks. Shallots (var. *aggregatum*) are also members of this family, while the non-bulbing "green onions," aka scallions, "spring" onions, and "bunching "onions," can be either *A. cepa* or *A. fistulosum* (aka Welsh onions). Generally, red onions are the mildest and are often consumed uncooked, white onions are somewhere in the middle, and yellow onions, with their high sulfur content, are the strongest and sharpest tasting, although a few types like Vidalias are notoriously sweet.

Although most onions can be grown from seed, I recommend purchasing sets – onion plants purposefully kept small over one season then encouraged into dormancy to be planted the next – from you favorite seed house, as they will shorten your growing season from up to 150 days in some cases to a far more manageable 60 to 75 days. Usually sold in bunches of 25 or 50, plant these in good, nitrogen-rich soil in hilled-up rows in a sunny position about 1 inch deep and 6 inches apart.

Let me recommend here a tasty summer side dish: toss quartered onions with olive oil, balsamic vinegar, salt, and pepper, bake at 375 degrees until nicely cara-melized; cool and then sprinkle with fresh thyme or oregano, and serve alongside a room-temperature roast.

Onion 'Egyptian Walking'

Orange

Citrus x sinensis

"Eating an orange
While making love
Makes for bizarre
enjoyment thereof."

—Tom Lehrer, American humorist, b. 1928

*D*NA evidence suggests our familiar sweet orange *(Citrus x sinensis)*, versus its bosom companion the sour bitter orange *(Citrus x aurantium)*, which has a bit of citron *(Citrus medica)* in its parentage, is a spawn of the pummelo *(Citrus grandis)* and the mandarin *(Citrus reticulata)*. The eminent Swiss botanist Augustin Pyramus de Candolle maintained in the nineteenth century that the Burmese Peninsula and southern China were their original homes, and oranges were certainly known in the Indo-Orient as long ago as 3000 B.C. It is interesting to note, however, that while classical botanists from Theophrastus right through Pliny make liberal mention of the citron, there is not a single mention of the orange. It is believed an orange of some sort was delivered into the Mediterranean by the Moors sometime before the ninth century A.D., and it is known that the warrior chieftain Al-Mansur, Muslim caliph of Andalusia, grew them in Cordoba, Spain, by A.D. 976. Marco Polo reported oranges under cultivation near the Strait of Hormuz in Iran in the thirteenth century, and in 1499 it is recorded that Louis XII was given a sweet orange tree as a wedding present by the Spanish queen Leonora of Castile. It was Sir Francis Carew of Beddington in Surrey who, in the late sixteenth century, introduced the first sweet oranges into England,

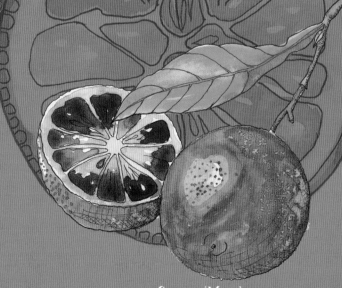

Orange 'Moro'

Orange 'Washington Navel'

John Evelyn recounting that "the oranges were planted in the open ground & secured in winter only by a Tabernacle of boards, & stoves, removable in summer." By the mid-seventeenth century, Europe had been swept by what can only be described as "sweet orange mania," and no royal parterre was complete without a lane flanked with potted specimens, John Parkinson reporting in 1629 that "some keepe them in great square boxes and . . . cause them to be rowled by trundles, or small wheeles under them to place them in a house or close gallerie for the winter time."

Christopher Columbus delivered the orange to Hispaniola on his second voyage in 1493, and Ponce de León carried them into Florida in 1521, but there is no evidence that either was a "sweet" type. Many taxonomists believe *Citrus* x *sinensis* did not enter North America until 1769, when it was introduced from Mexico to California's first Franciscan mission at San Diego by Padre Junipero Serra. However they arrived, in terms of health benefits, we're all keenly aware of the sweet orange's legendary content of vitamin C, but it is its impressive load of phytonutrients, including anthocyanins and polyphenols, that make it heroically antioxidant.

Some of our most notable orange varieties are the 'Navel', the 'Valencia', the 'Temple', and the beautiful, pink-blushed 'Blood' orange, and there are many more deserving of the attention of anyone in USDA zones 8 to 10 who might have the opportunity to culture some. For the rest of us, we should harken back to that antique habit of wheeling your prize orange tree out onto the patio when temperate climes descend and giving it a nice, sunny, sheltered spot in your home or greenhouse when temperatures drop. All oranges will reward you with glossy green foliage, heavenly scented, five-petaled white blossoms, and exceptional fruit, and an orange of any sunny hue is one of the few fruit plants that will achieve blossom and both ripe and unripe fruit all at once, for a truly show-stopping display.

John Parkinson comments in his *Paradisi in Sole Paradisus Terrestris* of 1629 that "orenges are used as a sawce for many sortes of meats, in respect of their sweete sowernesse, giving a rellish of delight, whereinsoever they are used," so why not a zesty, roasted fowl a l'orange this very night?

Oregano

Origanum spp., Plectranthus amboinicus 'Variegatus'

*Greek legend held that the sweet scent of oregano was created
by Aphrodite as a symbol of joy and, in parallel fable, the
Romans believed Venus left her perfume lingering in oregano
as a reminder of her beauty.*

As we have noted, the family *Origanum* is as vexatious a bunch of herbal personalities as one might chance to encounter, defiantly switching identity from oregano to marjoram and back again at will until one is simply tempted to throw up one's hands and head towards a nice, level-headed herb whose identity is steadfast. Although there are a number of *Origanum* constituents we here identify as oreganos, including Syrian or Egyptian oregano *(O. maru)*, and Spanish oregano *(O. vivens)*, in this section we will turn our attention to the main culinary type, "Greek" oregano *(O. vulgare hirtum)*, also, of course, called "winter marjoram," as well as an "oregano" of an entirely different but certainly winning plant form, *Plectranthus amboinicus,* known as both Cuban oregano and Mexican mint.

The ancient Greeks and Romans were wild fanciers of oregano, everyone from Theophrastus, Aristotle, and Hippocrates, to Dioscorides and Pliny revering it internally as a digestive aid, a stimulant, and a carminative, and externally and antiseptically for all manner of wounds, ulcers, and burns. And there was also that whole "joyful" idea (its Greek roots being *oros,* "mountain," and *ganos,* "joy," therefore "joy of the mountain"), and oregano was employed it all kinds of happiness-inducing ways: strewn on the floors of homes, stuffing pillows to induce sweet dreams, hung by doorways to ward off pestilence and evil, and crowning married couples to insure a blissful union.

We now know it is the phenols carvacrol, thymol, and rosmarinic acid as well as the flavonoids present in oreganos that add up to a truly phenomenal display of antiviral, antiseptic, anti-inflammatory, and antimicrobial power. In 2001, the USDA put 39 herbs to the antioxidant test, with oregano copping the crown, demonstrating 42 times more antioxidancy than an apple, 12 times more than an orange, and 4 times more than a blueberry. In addition, ample supplies of carvacrol, which gives these plants their camphor-like savor, can also be found in all the non-*Origanum* "oreganos," like the Cuban variety we will laud in a moment.

Oreganos can grow anywhere from 2 to 3 inches tall to a yard or more, with flower stems that may be erect or trailing, woody or non-woody, flowers that may be purple, pink, or white, and leaves that may be round, heart-shaped, elliptic, or oval, and hairy or smooth. As stated, the culinary champ *is O. vulgare hirtum,* aka Greek oregano, boasting grayish green leaves with white flowers on an erect stem and growing to about a foot tall. If you're going to hunt down a single variety to culture, that would be it, although there are very pretty golden, purple, and compact varieties as well. However, let me here turn your attention to variegated Cuban oregano *(Plectranthus amboinicus 'Variegata'),* as beautiful and savory a plant as one could ask for, with succulent green leaves vividly marginated in white, a lovely semi-vining habit, and possessing a marvelous savor somewhere between oregano and sage. Although an annual, the fleshy stems root in a thrice, grow like Topsy, and will be happy on a sunny windowsill all winter long. Culturally, the "true oreganos" are perennial, unfussy, and hardy to about USDA zone 5.

Italian cuisine would be impossible without oregano, so here I will urge you to the composition of a fresh pizza: crown some flatbreads with slices of fresh mozzarella and tomato, drizzle with a good olive oil, sprinkle with salt, pepper, and a handful of fresh oregano, and bake at 400 degrees until crisp and melt-y.

Cuban Oregano 'Variegata'

Parsley

Petroselinum crispum

*"This day from parsley bed, I'm sure, was dug my elder brother, Moore,
Had Papa dug me up before him, so many now would not adore him . . ."*

— John Hume, second son of the Earl of Marchmont
on the birthday of his brother, the heir, circa 1715

Parsley, yet another member of the *Umbelliferae* family and counting carrots, parsnips, celery, dill, and lovage among its edible cousins, is believed to be anciently native to the Mediterranean and the Middle East, with Carl Linneaus, Swedish author of binomial nomenclature, championing Sardinia; George Bentham, the noted nineteenth-century British botanist, the eastern Mediterranean; and Augustin Pyramus de Candolle, the Swiss botanist of the same century, Turkey, Algeria, and Lebanon. The principal varieties are our familiar curly-leaved (*Petroselinum crispum*) and flat-leaved (*P. crispum* var. *neapolitanum*) parsleys, Hamburg or broad-leaved parsley (*P. crispum* var. *tuberosum*), grown for its edible, parsnip-like root, and celery-leaved parsley (also *P. crispum* var. *neapolitanum*), grown for its edible, celery-like stalks. *Petroselinum*, parsley's binomial designation, bestowed on it by Dioscorides in the first century A.D., derives from the Greek *petros*, "rock," plus *selinon*, "celery," describing parsley's apparently historic predilection for rocky habitats.

Curly-leaved Parsley

130

Flat-leaved Parsley

In 322 B.C., Theophrastus described the two types we will be romancing here, one with "crowded, dense leaves," the curly-leaved variety, and the other with "more open and broad leafage," the flat-leaved (Italian) type. Oddly, parsley was both enjoyed and feared by the ancients, as, according to legend, the plant first sprouted from the bloody ground of the slain Greek king Archemorus, whose name translates to the rather depressing "forerunner of death," and the expression *De'eis thai selinon,* "to need only parsley," was the ancient Greek equivalent of "one foot in the grave." On the other hand, Pliny the Elder states in his *Naturalis Historia* of A.D. 77 that "not a salad or sauce" was presented without parsley, "for the sprays find use in large quantities in broths and give a peculiar palatability to condimental foods," and, in A.D. 164, Galen praises parsley as being both "sweet and grateful to the stomach." Gerard is of the same opinion, in 1597 stating that parsley is ". . . delightful to the taste and agreeable to the stomache," with Culpeper concurring in 1653, "It is very comfortable to the stomach . . . ," and adding that it is ". . . good for wind and to remove obstructions both of the liver and spleen." What we now know is that parsley is nicely high in vitamins A, B, and C, potassium, iron, chlorophyll, calcium, phosphorus, niacin, and riboflavin, and, while it has carminative, tonic, and laxative qualities, it is its diuretic and detoxifying properties that are its chief values.

Parsley, although biennial, is an easily cultured annual in most of our precincts, as, in any case, parsley beds need to be renewed every two years. Therefore, soak seeds of either type overnight before planting for optimal germination, then plant half an inch deep, ultimately thinning to about 6 inches apart. Bizarrely, parsley is said to be fatal to small birds, injurious to other fowl, and lethal to parrots, but it is complete ambrosia to hares and rabbits.

Flat-leaved parsley is thought to have a stronger flavor and slightly tougher consistency than the curly-leaved type, but both are indispensable in the kitchen, so my advice is plant up a pot or plot of each to decorate both your garden and your plates. It is entirely rarely that I send out a dish without a sprig or two of one or the other, for, as the British author Thomas Hill, aka Didymus Mountain, so aptly put it in 1577, "There is nothing that doth like sweeten the mouth, as fresh and green Parcely eaten."

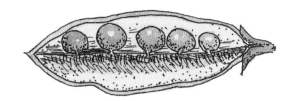

Pea

Pisum sativum

"The chapter of the pea endures always; the impatience to consume them, the pleasure of watching them be consumed, and the joy of consuming them again . . . It is a fashion and a furor."
—Madame de Maintenon, May 16, 1696

The origin of the wild pea is spectacularly obscure for being so early, but Ethiopia, the Mediterranean, and central Asia are usually mentioned. Charred pea remains have been recovered in Turkey dating from 7500 to 7000 B.C., found in Egyptian tombs of the Twelfth Dynasty, and, biblically, peas were among the foods brought to David in the desert (II Sam. 17:28). In fact, one can actually trace the expansion of Stone Age farming by the pea's carbonized remains as it traveled from Nea Nikomedia in Greece in 5500 B.C. to the Nile Delta in 5000 B.C., the western Mediterranean and India in 2000 B.C., and China somewhere between 916 and 618 B.C. A pot was discovered on the site of Homeric Troy containing 440 pounds of peas, and Theophrastus, friend of Aristotle and pupil of Plato, mentions peas in his third-century B.C. *Historia Planterum*.

Peas were the principal British food crop even before the Norman Conquests, and it was the Romans who most probably introduced the cultivated pea to Britain, although it wasn't until the early seventeenth century that a distinction was finally drawn between the "field" pea, which was dried then boiled later into "pease porridge," and the "green" pea, which was eaten green. John Gerard rather grumpily romances the ancient field pea in his *Herball* of 1597: "These Pease, which by their great increase did such good to the poore . . . without doubt grew there many years before, but were not observed till hunger made them take notice of them, and quickened their invention, which commonly in our people is very dull . . ." In 1660, "green" peas were introduced to the court of Louis XIV of France from Italy when the Savoyan Comte de Soissons, after some ostentatious throne-side shelling, presented small dishes of them to the king and queen. By 1696, when Mme. de Maintenon made her exasperated pronouncement, adding, "There are women who, after dining, and dining well, demand peas before sleeping at the risk of indigestion," they were the French culinary cat's meow. By 1800, Thomas Jefferson was planting thirty varieties at Monticello, and Vilmorin-Andrieux's *The Vegetable Garden*, published between 1850 and 1895 by that esteemed French seed house, devotes fifty pages to cultivated peas.

Contemporarily, peas should still be on everyone's edible plant list not only for their excellent swats of K, C, and B vitamins, fiber, phosphorous, and folate, but for their proprietary saponin content, which makes them, like all legumes, both wonderfully antioxidant and anti-inflammatory.

There are mainly three types of peas in the *P. sativum* clan: green peas *(Pisum sativum)*, snow peas (*Pisum sativum* var. *macrocarpon*) and sugar snaps (*Pisum sativum* var. *macrocarpon ser. cv.*). Some popular contemporary cultivars are 'Patriot', 'Early Perfection', 'Lincoln', and 'Survivor' in the green pea category, the snow peas 'Mammoth Melting', 'Oregon Sugar', and the sunny 'Golden Sweet', and the sugar snaps 'Sugar Bon', 'Cascadia', and 'Super Sugar'. Garden peas, of course, need to be shelled, while snow peas and sugar snaps are both prized for their eminently edible pods and slightly sweeter savor. All peas are cool-season vegetables and dedicated climbers, so plant out around a trellis or other support 1 inch deep and 3 or 4 inches apart in a sunny spot in early spring as soon as soil can be worked and you should be enjoying most types in 60 to 70 days. I recommend any of these lightly steamed and simply dressed with a knob of butter, some lemon juice, and some chopped fresh mint.

Snow Pea 'Golden Sweet'

Peach

Prunus persica

*Lao-Tzu, founder of Chinese Taoism, wrote of a
peach tree growing on the highest peak of the Kwun-lum
Mountains so tall, paradise rested in its branches.*

China is the antique birthplace of the peach, where they were considered the most sacred plant of the Taoist religion as far back as the tenth century B.C., *tao* actually translating to "peach." Despite its fuzzy familiarity, the peach is somewhat of a botanical mystery, being one of the few edible food plants that has never been identified in a truly wild state, indicating incredibly ancient culture in China. In Chinese legend, the peach grew in the goddess Hsi Wang Mu's garden, fruiting only once every 3,000 years and conferring eternal life on those who were lucky enough to merit a bite. By 300 B.C. the peach had been imported first into Persia and then into Greece, and by the first century A.D., it was under extensive cultivation in the Roman Empire. The peach was given its misguided *persica* designation in the third Century B.C. by Theophrastus, Greek father of botany, who erroneously believed that Persia was its country of origin.

The peach made its way into England and France in the sixteenth century and was first introduced into the New World in 1562 by French explorers near Mobile, Alabama. Native Americans are credited with moving the peach west across the United States with their seasonal migrations, and interestingly, in part because fairly any peach pit when planted will result in a tree, the early peach trees imported into the New World grew with such abandon that post-sixteenth-century settlers supposed them to be native to the Americas, William Penn recording in 1683 that dense native thickets of wild peach trees were full of fruit just north of Philadelphia.

Peach 'Indian Blood'

134

Peach 'Belle of Georgia'

As with all ancient edible plants, the peach figured in a variety of medicinal employments, Nicholas Culpeper reporting in his *Complete Herbal* of 1653 that "Venus owns this tree" and that "the fruit promotes lust." He also informs us that "nothing is better to purge choler and jaundice . . ." and that "if the kernels be bruised and boiled in vinegar . . . and applied to the head, it marvellously makes the hair to grow again upon bald places . . ." Modern medicine confirms that peaches are good sources of beta-carotene and vitamins A, B, and C as well as fiber, and are valued for their diuretic, digestive, and laxative properties.

There are over 2,000 varieties of peach, falling into three basic categories, depending on how firmly the flesh of the peach "clings" to the pit. "Clingstones" like 'Halford', 'Arctic Supreme', 'Ruby Prince', and the white-fleshed 'Camden' and 'Starlite' are generally softer and juicier and are so named because their flesh grips like a long-lost lover. "Freestones" like Harvester', 'Fireprince', 'Majestic', and the familiar 'Elberta' possess firmer, less juicy flesh that detaches easily from the stone. "Semi-freestones" like "Summerprince', 'Southern Pearl', and 'Coronet' are modern hybrids of the two other types, combining their best attributes of tender flesh and detachability.

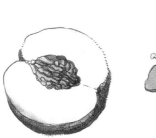

I will admit here, however, that, despite their profligacy in antique times, modern peach trees need a good deal of attention to fruit successfully. All will enjoy being pruned to an open center when young, have the fruit thinned to 1 peach to every 6 inches of limb after annual blooming, and a dormant oil spray will be helpful before blossoming as will a dose of fungicide and insecticide as your tree begins to develop fruit. Does this all sound like way too much chemistry and effort? To be honest, it is right on the cusp. But to pluck a warm peach off your own tree and sink your teeth into that honeyed flesh? You be the judge.

Pear

Pyrus communis

"The pear must be approached, as its feminine nature indicates, with discretion and reverence; it withholds its secrets from the merely hungry."

–Edward Bunyard, *The Anatomy of Dessert*, 1929

The genus *Pyrus*, encompassing about 22 separate species, is another absurdly ancient member of the greater rose *(Rosaceae)* family. Thought to be originally native to the northern Middle East, the wild pear, like many antique food plants, was a small, bitter, barely edible thing; however, culture of this antique food plant came very early on. As long ago as 5000 B.C., the Chinese diplomat Feng Li had famously given up his civil career to devote himself to the grafting of pears and other fruits, and it is known from carbon-dated seed remains that by 3500 B.C., the ancient lake dwellers of Switzerland were dallying with the pear. By the first century A.D., *Pyrus communis* cultivars had been divided by Pliny the Elder into two groups: the "proud" pears, so called because they fruited early and would not be "kept," and the "winter," or late, pears, which fruited in the fall and were generally used for cooking. Cato the Elder recorded 6 varieties in his *De Agri Cultura* of about 160 B.C. and Pliny a total of 41 in his *Naturalis Historia* of A.D. 77; by the early seventeenth century, Cosimo de' Medici II, grand duke of Tuscany, was offering his guests 209 different types; and by 1653, Nicholas Culpeper was commenting in his *Complete Herbal* that "Pear Trees are so well known, that they need no description."

In 1630, the first American pear seedling was delivered to Governor John Endicott in Salem, Massachusetts, and the 'Endicott' pear still stands in Danversport, Massachusetts, at an astonishing 385 years of age. However, unforeseen pome disaster struck in the guise of fireblight *(Erwinia amylovora)*, a bacterial infestation first reported in New York in 1793 that would kill pear trees outright; there is still no known cure and its occurrence is still completely erratic, decades passing without incident followed by weeks of abrupt annihilation. Thankfully, subsequent breeding of the Far Eastern Asian pear, or "sand pear" *(Pyrus pyrifolia)*, with its European cousins has produced a swarm of good-tasting, disease-resistant cultivars.

While pears, historically, were valued for both external and internal medicinal employments, ranging from typical wound-healing poultices to digestive health, modern science tells us that, aside from dietary fiber, pears offer oddly little in the way of health benefits, but don't let that incidental dissuade you as the following probably will.

Therefore, allow me to verge on the brusque: culturally, pears can be perfectly exasperating, and while some of the new hybrids like 'Ledbetter', 'Shenandoah', 'Magness', 'Moonglow', and 'Warren' are touted as being fireblight resistant or tolerant, many others, like the legendary continental variety 'Doyenne du Comice', are not, and there are no European pears varieties that are self-fruitful. Pears can also be exceedingly finicky about their time of harvest: too soon and they can be tasteless and coarse-fleshed, too late and they are little better than brown mush. As the great nineteenth-century transcendentalist philosopher Ralph Waldo Emerson so perceptively put it, "There are only ten minutes in the life of a pear when it is perfect to eat." Still, for a chance to sample one of these uniquely ambrosial fruits at that perfect moment, and to enjoy that beautiful flurry of white blossoms in spring, why not plant a couple of pear varieties that bloom and fruit at the same time for cross-pollination and do as Louis XIV did at Versailles: train them in a double or triple row on espalier wires as a fencelike feature in your garden, and hope for the best. If the best arrives, sink your teeth into it posthaste or, better yet, I can't think of a more appealing candidate for a grunt or crumble.

Pear 'Shenandoah'

Pepper 'Lemon Drop'   Pepper 'Fish'

Pepper

Capsicum annuum

*In 1550, the alarmist and clearly culinarily timid Flemish botanist
Rembert Dodoens announced that the hot peppers
recently introduced into Europe were strong enough to kill dogs.*

Although some botanists feel the pepper may have an ancient Caribbean prov-
enance, they are, basically, native to the American continent alone and are all
thought to be descendants of the native American bird pepper, which can still be
found growing in the wild. Whatever the case, they made their way into the southern
Americas extremely early in our prehistory, Aztec remains indicating dates as early
as 6500 B.C. Peppers were held in such high regard by the Aztec, Mayan, and Inca
cultures that they were objects of tribute, veneration, and even currency, and it was
hot peppers in particular, traveling homeward in the pockets of the gold-hungry
conquistadors, that took the world by storm as an alternative to the highly expensive
black pepper *(Piper nigrum)*, brought along the spice roads from India.

Hot peppers, both fresh and dried, have been used by native healers since the
dawn of medical employment for everything from joint pain to asthma, sore throats,
and yellow fever, and the American Medical Association still recommends ten drops of
hot pepper sauce in half a glass of water as an extremely effective sore throat remedy.
Additionally, ingested hot pepper has recently been shown to provide substantial

relief for certain kinds of chronic pain, and it is a fact that a teaspoon of dried hot pepper in hot water will stop a heart attack in progress. As well, people are mistaken in believing that hot peppers are irritants to the digestive system; in fact, members of the *Capsicum* family have quite the opposite effect, being both beneficial to digestion and soothing to the stomach. It's also interesting to note that a hot pepper can contain as much as six times the amount of vitamin C as in an orange, the highest level being found in the immature green fruit.

The heat in hot peppers involves a complex of compounds called capsaicinoids, and in 1912, American pharmacist Wilbur L. Scoville developed a method of measuring capsaicinoid content, sweet peppers, for instance, clocking in at 0 because they contain no capsaicinoids, while jalapeños score from 2,500 to 4,000 Scoville Units, Cayennes 60,000 to 80,000, Habañeros a tongue-tingling 200,000 to 300,000 units, Bhut Jolokia (cultivar Ghost Pepper) a truly fiery 1,041,427 units, with the Carolina Reaper at a mouth-deadening 1,569,300 units being the world's current hottest spice.

If it seems like we've been dwelling on the glory of the hot pepper to the detriment of our benign sweet pepper, we have been; so here we will stop to romance some of the sweet types. First of all, they are mighty good for you, too, particularly the deep-toned red, purple, and "chocolate" types, which are loaded with phytonutrients, some notable varieties being 'Ace', 'Olympus', 'Horizon Orange', 'Purple Beauty', 'Pequillo', and 'Jimmy Nardello'. As for the hot types, we always plant Habaneros, Cayennes, and Jalapenos and love the decorative varieties like the yellow-fruited 'Lemon Drop' and the variegated foliage cultivars 'Fish' and 'Trifetti', all adding both spice and health to our meals on the farm. Peppers are definitely tropicals but, that said, they are wonderfully carefree to culture, so start them in the greenhouse or your sunniest window 6 weeks prior to your frost date and plant out in June, spacing them 18 inches apart in a nice, sunny spot, and just watch them perform.

To make a simply splendid remedy for a sore throat, mix a teaspoon of any dried hot pepper with two of honey in your homiest mug, fill with hot water, and sip soothingly.

Pepper 'Cayenne'   Pepper 'Habañero'   Pepper 'Trifetti'

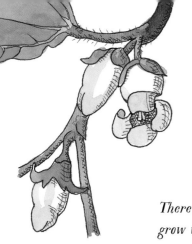

Persimmon

Diospyros kaki, D. virginiana

There is a saying in the American Southeast, where persimmons grow wild, that they are only "good for dogs, hogs, and possums."

Members of the greater *Ebenaceae* family, persimmons are of two main camps: the tiny American persimmon *(Diospyros virginiana)* and the larger, more familiar Oriental or Japanese *persimmon (Diospyros kaki)*. The Latin *Diospyros* optimistically translates to "grain of Jove," or, alternatively, "fruit of the gods," which certainly indicates antique adoration, and fossilized remains of the grape-sized, mouth-puckering American persimmon have been found in Greenland and Alaska dating to the Miocene Era, making them at least 5 million years old. They can still be found growing wild throughout Maryland, Virginia, and the Carolinas.

Although there are both astringent and non-astringent types in the Oriental camp, the American persimmon needs to be extremely ripe in order to be edible, Captain John Smith, who founded the first permanent English settlement in America at Jamestown, Virginia, in 1607, reporting, "If it be not ripe it will drawe a mans mouth awrie with much torment," but further adding, "but when it is ripe, it is as delicious as an Apricock." The key here, clearly, is "when it is ripe," as the tannin present in a mouthful of unripe American persimmon could probably remove paint from a car. Called *pasiminan* or *pessamin* by both the Algonquin Indians, who greeted the Jamestown settlers, and the Lenapes, with whom William Penn traded, history also records that during the Civil War, American persimmon seeds were boiled by soldiers of the Confederacy into a coffee-like beverage.

The larger, more familiar Oriental persimmon, despite being originally native to China, is universally identified with Japan and numbers about 2,000 different cultivars. It was Commodore Matthew Perry who, after bullying his way into Nagasaki Harbor and opening Japan to the West in 1854, returned to the United States with *Diospyros kaki* persimmon trees, also opening American eyes to the heights to which a persimmon might aspire. Persimmons of either family are excellent conduits of vitamins C and A, potassium, calcium, and iron, a number of important phytonutrients, and a smattering of B vitamins.

Persimmon 'Jiro'

Some of the most popular American persimmon varieties are 'Early Golden', 'Meader', 'Woolbright', 'Ennis', and 'Ruby', all being hardy to USDA zones 5 to 11 and all being large, attractive trees with shiny, magnolia-like leaves turning orange/red in autumn, an added visual bonus being that the fruit ripens after the leaves fall, so the trees look as if they are hung with glossy orange Christmas ornaments. The Oriental persimmons are divided into two über-camps: the brilliantly orange, acorn-shaped, highly astringent Hachiya, which dominates the commercial market and, like the American persimmon, is only edible when fully ripe, and the Fuyu type, also bright orange but squatter and famously non-astringent, the 'Jiro' cultivar, in particular, being so docile in personality that it may be eaten crisp like an apple. Both of these boast smaller, prettier habits than their American cousins, although they are hardy only to USDA zone 7.

Persimmons can grow to anywhere from 15 to 40 feet, so they will need some sunny space, and are, typically, either male or female, so most will need a cross pollinator, although in this apparently free-wheeling clan, some may produce both types of flowers or their sexual expression may vary from year to year. As we have noted perhaps to the point of boredom, most persimmons need to be extremely ripe to be edible, but when they are, all you will need to enjoy their sweet, spicy savor are a knife and a spoon. Do, however, allow them to languish a while in a silver bowl on a highly polished wooden surface to give you a bit of a visual feast first.

Pineapple

Ananas comosus

Love is like a pineapple,
sweet and undefinable.

—Piet Hein, "What Love is Like," 2002

*T*he pineapple, a member of the *Bromeliad* family, is an ancient American food plant native to southern Brazil and Paraguay, domesticated in pre-Columbian times in the Orinoco and Amazon River basins, and it was probably the sea-venturing Guaraní Indians who dispersed the plants from their native Paraguay throughout South and Central America and the West Indies. In an odd duality of sentiment, it is known that early West Indians planted hedges of prickly pineapples around their villages to keep out intruders while, at the same time, hanging them at their gates to signify welcome and abundance. This latter connotation was adopted by the fifteenth- and sixteenth-century Spanish explorers who carried it back to the Old World, and the pineapple, originally *a-nana*, Caribbean for "fruit" and "excellent," has forever after been symbolic of the twin qualities of bounty and hospitality.

It is Christopher Columbus who is responsible for both the pineapple's current appellation – calling the exotic fruit *piña* because it looked like a pinecone – and its introduction into Europe in 1493. Pineapples remained a rarity destined only for aristocratic tables until 1686, when a Dutch grower, M. Le Cour, successfully cultured the first European pineapples under glass. By the 1690s, all of Europe was lauding them as the horticultural *debutante du jour,* and pineapples became so important a symbol of affluence and welcome in the early American colonies that hospitable households would rent one for a day, and then return it to the grocer to be sold to someone who could actually afford to consume it. The pineapple we know today first appeared at the turn of the eighteenth century, after improvement by the ever-industrious Dutch. By 1835, there were 52 varieties listed in Europe, and, by 1856, 70.

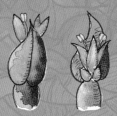

As Bromeliads, pineapples are spiky, sword-leaved plants from which a single stem and fruit rises centrally, although the pineapple is technically not a single fruit at all, but a "sorosis" – a cluster of tiny flowers growing on the plant's spike, each flower ultimately engorging with pulp to form the flesh and one of the meaty "scales" of the pineapple's exterior.

Pineapple 'Smooth Cayenne'

Pineapples are an excellent source of manganese and vitamins C and B1, as well as bromelain, an enzyme with a promising future in the treatment of heart attacks, abscesses, and ulcers. There are two main commercial varieties: the painfully serrated 'Red Spanish' and the 'Smooth Cayenne', with both a larger and more elongated shape, sweet, deep yellow flesh, and leaves with a smooth, nonthreatening edge, which is why I propose it to you here. First selected and cultivated in Venezuela, the 'Smooth Cayenne' was introduced from Cayenne (French Guiana) into Europe in 1820, eventually reaching the Royal Botanical Gardens at Kew in England, where it was improved and ultimately distributed to Jamaica, Australia, and Hawaii, as it is only truly hardy to USDA zones 10 and 11.

However, the culture of a pineapple top is one of those horticultural diversions familiar to any schoolchild and is riotously amusing when it finally pays off, which is why I recommend it to you here. To do so, just cut the top inch of crown off a store-bought pineapple, scoop the flesh out of the hollow, and plant shallowly in a pot of well-aerated soil. Keep it moist and warm and in as much sun as is possible, and your pineapple top will root within weeks, leaf becomingly, flower in about 18 months, and triumphantly fruit about 6 months after that. I believe this is another fantastic salsa idea in the making (lime, cilantro, jalapeño, sweet onion)—perhaps after displaying your pineapple in some place of pride or renting it, briefly, to one of your less well-to-do neighbors.

Plum

Prunus domestica, P. salicina

"Little Jack Horner sat in the corner
Eating his Christmas pie,
He put in his thumb and pulled out a plum
And said 'What a good boy am I!"

—Traditional English rhyme, eighteenth century

*L*et's get this "Little Jack Horner" thing out of the way first. "Jack," far from being exemplary, was actually one Thomas Horner, sixteenth-century steward to Richard Whiting, Catholic abbot of Glastonbury. In 1540, during Henry VIII's dissolution of the monasteries, Whiting sent Horner to London with a Christmas pie in which were concealed the deeds of a dozen manors, which the abbot hoped might assuage the newly Protestant monarch. On the journey, Horner extracted for himself the "plum" of the deed to the manor of Mells in Somerset and betrayed the abbot to the king, a contemporaneous rhyme commenting: "Hopton, Horner, Smyth and Thynne: When Abbotts went out, they came in." So much for "Jack" being a good boy.

144

Now, there are many types of plums but only two main contenders in the "fresh edible" category: *Prunus domestica,* the European plum, and *Prunus salicina,* called the "Japanese" plum, although it is actually native to China. Stones from *Prunus domestica* have been unearthed at Maiden Castle in Dorset, England, dating to a very impressive eighth-century B.C., and mentions of *Prunus salicina* make frequent appearances in the fifth-century B.C. songs and writings of Confucius, the Japanese plum also being anciently associated with great age, wisdom, and good fortune. By the first century A.D., Pliny the Elder was noting of the European plum and its 300 known varieties that "no other tree has been so ingeniously crossed," and it is known that "Japanese" plums were under domestication in Japan at approximately the same moment the European plum entered the New World with the first English settlers. George Washington is known to have planted "three amber Plumbs . . ." at Mount Vernon on February 27, 1786, and Japanese plums were introduced into the United States in about 1870, when they entered California from the Orient. Plums of both families are beyond impressive in terms of their antioxidant performance, being fantastic sources of vitamins C and A and particularly effective in neutralizing the notoriously destructive "superoxide anion" oxygen radical.

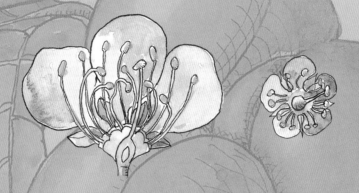

As noted, there are scores of plum varieties of every pretty hue coming to us from many points on the globe, from the deep purple Damsons and the luscious green Greengages of British lore to the red-skinned Japanese Satsumas and the golden French Mirabelles. However, it is to America's most famous breeder of plants, Luther Burbank, I will direct you now, as starting in 1885, he began hybridizing the *Prunus salicina* with the climatically hardy but far less tasty native American types (*P. americana, P. hortulana, P. nigra,* and *P. maritima*) with fantastic results, increasing hardiness, disease resistance, and taste, and all currently available hybrids are descendants of his progeny. Some of these broadly feted darlings are 'Superior', 'Underwood', 'Alderman', 'Pipestone', and 'Black Ice', but my advice is to consult your local nurseries for the best choices for your zone and climate. All plums will reward you with lovely small, spreading trees, brilliant green foliage, and fragrant, five-petaled, white to deep pink flowers, and most will be hardy in USDA zones 5 to 9. Most plums are not self-fertile so you will need to plant a companion for cross-pollination, and all types will require some pruning, enjoy being trained to an open center, and will benefit from some blossom thinning as well as some pest and blight application for optimal fruit production.

In deference to the misused ancient abbot of Glastonbury, here I will suggest the composition of a nice plum tart and a smart thumbing of the nose to that devious "Jack."

Potato
'Adirondack Blue'

Potato

Solanum tuberosum, Ipomoea batatas

*"Only two things in this world are too serious to be jested on,
potatoes and matrimony."*

–Irish saying

Our subjects in this chapter, the potato *(Solanum tuberosum)* and the sweet potato *(Ipomoea batatas)*, come to us from two different species but, oddly, exactly the same spot on the globe, the earliest documented remains of both having been found in Peru, the sweet potato dating to about 8000 B.C. and the potato to 2500 B.C., by which date the sweet potato seems to have entered the Caribbean. The sweet potato then journeyed on to Polynesia and the Cook Islands by A.D. 1000, and it was Christopher Columbus who delivered them to the Old World and Spain in 1492. The *Solanum* types are thought to have been introduced into Europe in 1567, when Juan de Molina sent two barrels from the Canary Islands to his brother in Antwerp, Belgium, and it was either Sir Walter Raleigh or Sir Francis Drake who introduced them to Ireland and England about twenty years after that, the inscription on a statue of Sir Francis in Offenburg, Germany, reading, "Sir Francis Drake, disseminator of the potato in Europe in the Year of Our Lord 1586. Millions of people who cultivate the earth bless his immortal memory."

The *Solanums* arrived in North America in 1621 when Nathaniel Butler, governor of Bermuda, sent some to Francis Wyatt, governor of Virginia, and it was Scotch-Irish immigrants who undertook their first U.S. cultivation in Londonderry, New Hampshire, in 1719. By 1785, the French journal *Bon Jardinier* was reporting of the potato, "There is no vegetable about which so much has been written and so much enthusiasm has been shown," and by the nineteenth century, potatoes had superseded every grain crop in Europe due to three nearly deific advantages: sheer caloric and nutrient bulk, lower rate of spoilage, and inexpensive cost of culture, the Marxist philosopher Friedrich Engels declaring that the potato rivaled the discovery of iron in playing a "historically revolutionary role."

However, famously and disastrously, from 1845 to 1849, potato blight *(Phytophthora infestans)* decimated the Irish crop, resulting in the Great Irish Potato Famine, nearly one million deaths, and the mass exodus of a million more Irish citizens to the United States and Canada. Today, the potato continues its reign as the world's fifth most important food crop, most varieties being excellent sources of vitamins C and B, important phytochemicals, phosphorus and potassium, while the orange-fleshed sweet potato offers up extremely healthy loads of vitamins A and B, beta-carotene, and a good smattering of minerals.

There are literally scores of varieties of potatoes in a vast range of profiles, sizes, and colorations, so, again, the best that I can do here is enumerate some of our historic favorites on the farm. Our personal preference is to grow the smaller varieties like 'Yukon Gold', the pink-skinned heirlooms 'Rose Finn' and 'French Fingerling', and the colorful purple and blue-fleshed types like 'Purple Majesty' and 'Adirondack Blue'. We have never cultured sweet potatoes, as they need at least three months of blistery temperatures to perform well; but should you be able to accommodate them, some popular varieties are 'Hernandez', 'Jewel', 'Covington', and 'Centennial'. Sweet potatoes are cultured from "slips," young greenhouse-grown shoots, and potatoes from "seeds," potato bits that contain at least one eye, available from most seed houses. Potatoes are ready to dig when their foliage starts to die back, and do let them "cure" in the sun for a few days before employment.

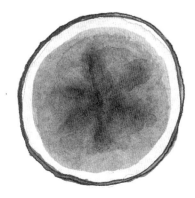

Pumpkin

Cucurbita pepo

"For pottage and puddings and custard and pies,
Our pumpkins and parsnip are common supplies:
We have pumpkins at morning and pumpkins at noon,
If it were not for pumpkins, we should be undoon!"

—American Pilgrim verse, circa 1633

*T*he pumpkin is one of our oldest native American crops, pumpkin seeds having been found at Machu Picchu and the Oaxaca Highlands in Mexico and in the caves of the basket-weaving tribes of Colorado and Arizona dating from between 2000 and 5000 B.C. Native Americans believed pumpkins had been brought to earth by the Maize Mother, who walked the fields and plains in human form, causing maize to grow from her footsteps and pumpkins and squash plants to sprout in her wake.

In 1529, Hernando de Soto reported from Tampa Bay, Florida, that "beans and pumpkins were in great plenty . . . the pumpkins when roasted had nearly the taste of chestnuts." As we all know, pumpkins were also among the foodstuffs served at the Pilgrims' first Thanksgiving, and, in fact, for many years, members of the Church of England referred to Thanksgiving derisively as "St. Pompion's Day," *pompion* being the Old English nomenclature for the pumpkin. Edward Johnson, in his *Wonder Working Providence of Scions Saviour in New England* of 1654, wrote that the pumpkin was

Pumpkin 'Baby Boo'

Pumpkin 'Jarrahdale'

"a fruit which the Lord fed his people with till corn and cattle increased," and the pumpkin was so widely regarded as a food crop in the Massachusetts colonies that Boston, before it was called Beantown, was known as Pumpkinshire. By 1780, Yale students were referring to all New Englanders as "Pumpkin Heads," another derisive term derived from the law that required men's haircuts to conform to a cap placed over the head, the ubiquitous pumpkin shell often, apparently, being substituted for the far scarcer caps.

Size also seems to have been a lifelong issue with the pumpkin in America, as in 1699, Massachusetts farmer Paul Dudley boasted of having produced a specimen weighing 260 pounds, and in 1721, the diarist Joshua Hempstead of New London, Connecticut, noted, "Wednesday, 20th: saw a pumpkin 5 foot 11 inches round."

Pumpkins are one of nature's greatest sources of beta-carotene and Vitamin A, 100 grams offering up a fantastic 246 percent of your daily requirement, plus 15 percent of vitamin C, 14 percent of copper, 10 percent of iron, and healthy doses of those free radical scavengers lutein and zeaxanthin. As for pumpkin seeds, 100 grams will give you plenty of fiber plus 110 percent of your daily dose of iron, 31 percent of niacin, and 71 percent of zinc.

We are all familiar with those large, bright orange denizens of fright nights and ghoulish doings come October, but the earliest pumpkin cultivars were probably gourd-necked, small, and bitter tasting. Pumpkins are contemporarily available in a vast array of sizes and colorations, the common Jack O'Lantern type most probably being the venerable 'Connecticut Field' pumpkin; but others that might be of interest are the delightfully diminutive and ghostly white 'Baby Boo', the historic American favorite 'Long Island Cheese', the ancient French 'Rouge Vif d'Etampes', the gorgeous blue/gray Australian 'Jarrahdale', and the equally entrancing knobby-skinned Italian 'Marina di Chioggia'. The size of the variety you choose to culture will dictate your spatial requirements, but be forewarned: pumpkins, like melons, take up a lot of real estate. All will grow best in a rich soil with some compost or manure worked into it, so, after your frost date, plant 3 seeds together 1 inch deep in hills 5 feet apart, thinning to the single best plant. Harvest in about 100 to 130 days depending on cultivar.

It would be unkind here not to honor both our forefathers and their hospitable native hosts with anything less than a fragrant pumpkin pie.

Quince

Cydonia oblonga

*"There is no fruit growing in the land that is of so many
excellent uses . . . serving as well to make many
dishes . . . and much more for their physical virtues."*

—John Parkinson, *Paradisi in Sole Paradisus Terrestris*, 1629

The quince is, physically, so close to its *Rosaceae* cousins the pear and the apple that it was once classified as a *Pyrus* but is now the only species in the genus *Cydonia*. Antiquely native to Persia and Mesopotamia, the Mediterranean quince, *Cydonia oblonga*, is puzzlingly classified as an entirely different genus from its decorative Asian cousins *(Chaenomeles speciosa, C. japonica, C. chinensis)*. Many feel it was the sunny-skinned *Cydonia oblonga* that constituted the "golden apples" of Greek myth, and it is also a popular contender in that whole fruit of Eden brouhaha. We know the Greeks imported improved varieties from Cydon in Crete – thus the derivation of this fruit's botanical name, and Columella, in his *De Re Rustica* of the

Quince

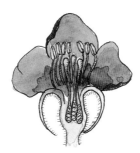

first century A.D., describes three varieties: the "sparrow apple," the "golden apple," and the "must apple." At approximately the same moment, Marcus Gavius Apicius, debatably the author of *De Re Coquinaria,* the world's first cookbook, recommended quinces boiled with honey and wine; Charlemagne introduced the quince into France in A.D. 812; Joan of Arc was known to have received a gift of cotignac, a jellied confection made from quince, when she arrived in Orleans in 1429; and Wynkyn de Worde, in his English *Boke of Kervynge* of 1509, aside from worryingly recommending that one "fruche that chekyn," also glows about "char de Quynce," the antique name for quince marmalade.

In the New World, quince's brief popularity in seventeenth-century New England waned quickly, as in colder climates the fruit is inedible raw, with a tough-ish, fuzzy skin and a hard, unpleasant flesh. Therefore, with the advent of more immediately accommodating fruit types like the apple and pear, the quince made a quiet exit from the American cultural scene. That is decidedly unfortunate, as there is absolutely nothing prettier than the gracefully gnarly, sculptural form of a quince tree, most notably in spring blossom, and the fruits are excellent when cooked – particularly, into that gorgeous, signature pink jelly.

Additionally and medicinally, the esteemed seventeenth-century English physician Sir Thomas Browne lauded the quince as "the stomach's comforter," and we know now that quinces are nicely high in vitamins C and B2, potassium, potash, and phosphorus.

As noted, there are two different species of quince: the edible *Cydonias* and the decorative *Chaenomeles,* and, as this is a tome about edible plants, here we will veer towards the *Cydonias,* while giving praise in passing to the flowering *Chaenomeles,* which, while they do fruit, are decidedly inferior to their *Cydonia* cousins in terms of edibility but are memorably decorative, particularly *C. speciosa* 'Contorta'. Some of the most popular *Cydonias* currently cultured are 'Angers', 'Orange', 'Pineapple', 'Champion', and 'Smyrna', the last being prized for the uniquely non-woolly, thin, smooth skin of its fruits.

Growing from 12 to 20 feet, with attractive green foliage turning a superb yellow to crimson in fall, quinces are adaptable to a wide range of soils and temperatures, are hardy in zones 5 to 9, and will reward you with lovely white-to-pink blossoms resembling old-fashioned single roses, followed by that pretty golden fruit.

As noted, in our precincts, raw quinces are inedible and are always cooked and sweetened, often into the easiest, prettiest, and most delicious of jellies because of their high pectin content. Therefore, boil washed, cored, and quartered quinces in a big pot, mash and strain, add just under a cup of sugar for every cup of juice rendered, re-boil till thickened, and jar. You'll be happy you did.

Rat-tail Radish

Radish

Raphanus sativus

"Radishes . . . were indeed by Dioscorides and Pliny celebrated
above all roots whatsoever; insomuch as in the Delphic
Temple . . . there was Raphanus ex auro discatus, a Radish of solid
Gold..."

–John Evelyn, *Acetaria: A Discourse of Sallets*, 1699

Although the birthplace of the radish is somewhat murky due to its extreme antiquity across many cultures, most botanists believe it evolved in the eastern Mediterranean from the wild *R. raphanistrum,* although it was an important food crop in Egypt by 2000 B.C. and was known in China as early as 1100 B.C. Actually a member of the mustard clan grown for its root rather than for its greens or seeds, *radish* derives from the Latin *radix,* meaning "root," and in its most ancient form, this peppery food plant is virtually indistinguishable from its wild ancestor. The antique Greeks esteemed the radish so highly that, as John Evelyn reports, solid gold replicas were placed in Apollonian temples as objects of devotion, while beets and turnips had to be content with replication in the baser metals of silver and lead. Both Dioscorides and Pliny the Elder noted the radish in the first century A.D., Dioscorides writing that the wild radish has "leaves like those of the cultivated . . . and a slender root, tender and subacrid . . . ," while Pliny the Elder attests that the "Syrian" variety " . . is pretty nearly the mildest and most tender of all."

Although we are mainly familiar with the small, round, red-skinned types, radishes can, in fact, vary in coloration from red to white, yellow, purple, and black and can run the gamut from the tiny and globular to the huge and parsnip-like. Ancient Greco-Roman legend tells of radishes weighing 50 pounds or more, ancient Jewish lore relates the tale of a radish so large that a fox hollowed it out and made a den of it, and, contemporarily, some of the Asian Daikons can grow to a truly impressive 3 feet in length.

Radish 'Misato Rose'

In medieval Europe, radish-based concoctions were directed for sore throats and congestive ailments, as well as for bouts of the more esoteric realms of madness and demonic possession. Reaching England in the sixteenth century, by the turn of the eighteenth, Tournefort's *Complete Herbal* was reporting of British herbalist John Parkinson in the seventeenth that "Parkinson sowed the seeds of this species, which produced plants, some of which had black roots; but the greater part had white skin . . ." Although they are, honestly, not wildly healthful sources of nutrients, modern medicine tells us that radishes contain good amounts of both ascorbic and folic acids, potassium, and vitamin B6, and a decoction is still recommended for throat complaints.

Some interesting modern cultivars to consider are the classic 'Early Scarlet Globe', the modern cultivar 'Cherry Belle', the elongated 'White Icicle', the wonderfully green-skinned and -fleshed 'Chinese Green Luobo', the Japanese 'Minowase' Daikon, the gorgeous pink-fleshed 'Misato Rose', and the classic French heirloom 'French Breakfast'. As well, there are fantastic radishes grown for their seedpods alone, like the evocatively named Rat-Tail Radish (var. *caudatus*), an ancient European probably via Asia variety with long, thin, curly, crunchy pods borne above ground and beautiful, edible, purple-tinged flowers.

Radishes are definitely cool-weather crops and wonderfully quick to germinate, so sow seed thinly about ½ inch deep in early spring as soon as ground can be worked and again in midsummer, thinning to 6 inches apart, and you should be harvesting in 35 to 55 days. I suggest enjoying radishes as the French do: fresh from the garden with a quick rinse, a dish of coarse salt, and another of softened, unsalted butter. Grab one by the leaves, dip into the butter, then the salt, and enjoy a wonderful, spring-y symphony of taste and texture.

Raspberry 'Amity'

Raspberry

Rubus idaeus

"Twas only to hear the yorling sing,
And pu' the crawflower round the spring,
The scarlet hep and the hindberrie,
And the nut that hang frae the hazel tree."

—Sixteenth-century British verse

Historically and famously, the raspberry has been associated with the two anciently sacred Mounts Ida, one purportedly their birthplace near the site of the ancient city of Troy in what is now Turkey, the other the highest point on the isle of Crete and, legendarily, boyhood home to Zeus. Consequently, the raspberry was widely known as the "Bramble of Mount Ida" in the Greek *Batos Idaia* and in the Latin *Rubus Idaea*, which Carl Linnaeus ultimately adopted as its botanical appellation. Raspberry remains have been found in the lake settlements of Switzerland dating to as long ago as 4000 B.C., but there are also both red and black raspberry varieties (*R. strigosus* and *R. occidentalis*) native to North America, and it is supposed that these were delivered there by travelers or animals crossing the Bering Strait in some equally misty predawn of time.

However, oddly, raspberry cultivation is not mentioned anywhere until Palladius's *Opus agriculturae* of the late fourth or early fifth century A.D., the plain fact being that the raspberry has grown like a prickly thug in every nation's ditch and hedgerow for so long, no one thought them worth domesticating until Palladius reported on their cultivation. It was the Romans who dispersed the raspberry throughout Europe, and by 1597, the English herbalist John Gerard was glowing about them, calling them "hindberrie," from the ancient Saxon *hindbeer*, with Nicholas Culpeper commenting in his *Herball* of 1653 that "the fruit has a pleasant grateful smell and taste, is cordial and strengthens the stomach, stays vomiting and is good to prevent miscarriage." Native Americans employed a tisane extracted from boiled raspberry leaves to treat pregnancy-related ailments, as well as diarrhea, stomach upset, lung congestion, and sore throat, and raspberry vinegar is still prescribed for fever, sore throats, and "complaints of the chest." Additionally, the usually deep-hued raspberry is a significant source of vitamin C, manganese, and fiber as well as anthocyanins and ellagic acid, an important free radical scavenger.

Raspberries are, technically, not berries at all, but "aggregate fruits," i.e., clusters of "drupelets," each tiny drupelet containing one seed and growing over a fleshy center "receptacle." When picked, the raspberry will detach from the receptacle, unlike a blackberry, which will detach with its receptacle intact.

Also, let's get this "ever" and "fall-bearing" thing straight: an "ever-bearing" habit is encouraged by cutting back all second-year canes (floracanes) to the ground and shortening all first-year canes (primocanes) to about 2 feet in fall. This will result in a small spring crop on the bottom of next year's floracanes, and an impressive fall crop on the tops of the new primocanes. Alternately, you can treat an "ever-bearing" variety as a single-crop "fall-bearing" type by cutting back all canes and allowing new primocanes alone to grow in spring. Some excellent modern cultivars are 'Amity', the Korean 'Fall Gold', 'Heritage', 'Titan', 'Ruby', 'Crimson Giant', and the European imports 'Autumn Bliss', and 'Himbo Top'. However, this is another instance when some consultation with your local nursery in terms of recommended types for your zone and conditions will not go unrewarded. All raspberries are hardy in USDA zones 3 through 9, are nicely self-fertile, and, beyond a bit of summer weeding and that necessary cane pruning at the end of the season, are as tough as pig iron.

A very useful thing to do with whatever variety you choose would be to put up some soothing raspberry vinegar: heat 1 ½ cups white vinegar with 1 cup raspberries and ½ cup sugar until fully dissolved, strain, bottle, and sip for what ails you.

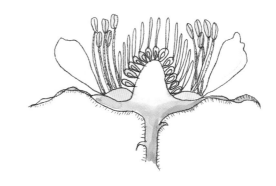

Raspberry 'Fall Gold'

Rhubarb

Rheum rhabarbarum, R. rhaponticum, R. officinale

Rhubarb is a very odd food plant indeed, as, for one thing, while its petioles (stalks) are famously edible, the oxalic acid content in its leaves is nearly lethal. For another, until well into the eighteenth century, rhubarb was not considered a food plant at all, but a purely medicinal one. Numbering about 60 species, the most notable *Rheums* are our familiar garden rhubarb *(R. rhabarbarum)*, "false" rhubarb *(R. rhaponticum)*, and Oriental medicinal rhubarb *(R. officinale)*. Some authorities attest *Rheum* derives from the Greek *rheo*, "to flow," in allusion to rhubarb's purgative properties, while the nineteenth-century English botanist John Lindley believed it originated in *Rha*, the ancient name for the Volga River in Russia, on whose banks it has grown since man had gills.

The earliest literary allusion to rhubarb dates to China and 2700 B.C., in reference to the medical applications of *R. officinale,* which somewhat later in history also success-fully assuaged the fever of the Wu Emperor of the Liang Dynasty (A.D. 464–549), and miraculously cured the Guangdong Emperor of the Song Dynasty (A.D. 1147–1200) of the "severe illness" he contracted after having had "a joyful time with four beautiful women." A further point of oddity concerning rhubarb, and specifically *R. officinale,* is the unusual zeal with which all of Europe sought to culture it, only to be abjectly disap-pointed. It seems that no matter what cultural niceties and varieties were pursued, no plant grown outside of Oriental rhubarb's native habitat managed to live up to the original, which, of course, made Europe crave it all the more. In fact, in the eighteenth century, the elusive *R. officinale* became such a pan-European obsession, it was remu-neratively traded by the East India Company in mind-boggling quantity. Some type of rhubarb is recorded in Italy by 1608, by 1640 it had spread into northern Europe, and by 1777, cultivation of *R. rhaponticum* in particular had commenced in Banbury, England, with seed procured from Russia.

An unidentified Maine gardener seems to have carried rhubarb into America sometime between 1790 and 1800, and by 1822, when its non-medicinal possibilities had begun to be considered, several types were available in markets. Medicinally, we know now that rhubarb is a good source of dietary fiber, vitamins K and C, calcium, potassium, and magnesium, as well as polyphenolic antioxidants like beta-carotene, lutein, and zeaxanthin, but it should be shunned by people with kidney problems due to the oxalic acid issue.

As our concentration is on edible plants, here we will leap the fence to embrace our familiar "garden-variety" rhubarb, *R. rhabarbarum*, some of the most popular contemporary cultivars being 'MacDonald', 'Victoria', 'Mammoth Red', 'Sunrise', 'Ruby', 'Crimson Red', and 'Valentine'. Rhubarbs are truly handsome plants of an almost prehistoric personality with immense crowns of green to pink to red petioles, every brawny stalk capped with a large, frilly if sadly un-good-for-you green leaf, with some varieties growing to a stately 4 or 5 feet, and once planted, most will remain productive for 8 to 15 years.

In honor of John Cleese and Monty Python, I will end this chapter with a classic rhubarb tart recipe: dissolve 1 cup sugar in ⅓ cup water, add some lemon peel, a cinnamon stick, and 6 cups of trimmed, sliced rhubarb stalks; bring to a boil, reduce heat, cover, and simmer until rhubarb softens. Remove from heat, cool, arrange the rhubarb bits in a baked tart shell brushed with apricot jam, strain the rhubarb liquid and re-boil until reduced to ¼ cup, cool again, spoon over the rhubarb, let set, and serve with fresh whipped cream.

Rhubarb

Rosemary

Rosmarinus officinalis

"Rosemary's for remembrance, between us day and night,
Wishing I may always have you present in my sight."
–Clement Robinson, "A Nosegay for Lovers," 1584

Rosemary is another member of the greater *Lamiaceae* (mint) family, native to mainly coastal locales in southern Europe and the Mediterranean, and Lady Rosalind Northcote says of this aromatic plant in *The Book of Herbs* of 1914, "Rosemary has always been of more importance than any other herb, and more than most of them put together."

Rosemary derives from the Latin botanical designation *Ros marinus*, meaning "dew of the sea," a reference to this shrubby herb's glistening leaves and seaside habit. In the first and second centuries A.D., Pliny the Elder, Dioscorides, and Galen all applauded rosemary's ability to "improve memory," and it was as a potent symbol of ritual "remembrance" that rosemary was widely regarded historically. Saint Thomas More, writing in the sixteenth century, reported, "As for Rosmarine . . .it is the herb sacred to remembrance, and, therefore, to friendship . . .," and Shakespeare's Ophelia significantly opines, "There's rosemary, that's for remembrance." In 1629, John Parkinson advised the use of rosemary "at wedding, funerals, etc. to bestow among friends . . ." with the seventeenth-century British poet Robert Herrick elaborating in verse, "Grow it for two ends, it matters not at all, / Be't for my bridal or my burial." In 1607, Roger Hacket, the distinguished English clergyman, sermonized, "Let this rosmarinus, this flower of men ensigne of your wisdom, love and loyaltie, be carried not only in your hands, but in your hearts and heads," and rosemary was characteristically entwined into bridal coronets, Anne of Cleves, the fourth of Henry VIII's six wives, having been known to sport one to her short-lived union. Rosemary served double duty at funerals, mourners carrying sprigs of it to ward off any noxious fumes that might be emanating from the corpse, then tossing the sprigs into the grave as a gesture of love and fidelity.

In *The Complete Herbal* of 1653, Culpeper commends rosemary for ". . . drowsiness or dulness of the mind and senses like a stupidness . . .benumbed joints, sinews, or members . . .a stinking breath . . ." and "to comfort the heart, and to expel the contagion of the pestilence." However, in 1814, we come up against Robert Thornton's celebrated *Herbal,* and this cruelly decisive rosemary truth: "This plant . . .has obtained a celebrity which it little merits . . ." and "has no claim to the high encomiums bestowed upon this simple herb." What we know now is that rosemary mainly contains volatile camphorous oil as well as nice doses of iron, calcium, and vitamin B6, and today the rendered oil is principally employed aromatherapeutically and as a fragrant stimulant in liniments.

Rosemary

In terms of cultivars, my experience had been that, unless you culture from seed, your local nursery will pretty much offer up a single variety of rosemary, usually that general crowd pleaser 'Tuscan Blue', although there are plenty of others to commend, like the blue-flowering beauties 'Blue Spires', 'Blue Lady', and 'Taylor's Blue', the white-flowering 'Alba', the chartreuse-leaved 'Joyce DeBaggio', the procumbens types like 'Mrs. Howard's Creeping', and those cold-climate stalwarts 'Arp' and 'Madelene Hill', which are reportedly hardy to USDA zone 5. Being denizens of the Mediterranean, however, most rosemary cultivars will like it sunny, hot, and dry but, that said, are wonderfully easy care in the correct situation, growing in some perennial cases into gloriously fragrant 6- or 7-foot shrubs.

Let me leave you here with this cool-weather idea: there's nothing more comforting than a big pan of roasted potatoes or root vegetables tossed with chopped rosemary, garlic, and olive oil of a blustery night.

Sage

Salvia officinalis, S. elegans

"Cur morietur homo cui Salvia crescit in horto?"
("How can a man die who grows sage in his garden?")
–Motto of the medical school of Salerno, Italy, eighth century A.D.

*A*nother member of the extensive *Lamiaceae* (mint) family, there are over 750 varieties of sage scattered around the globe, consisting of annuals, biennials, and perennials, our familiar garden sage *(Salvia officinalis)* hailing from the Mediterranean and Asia Minor, although it has been cultivated in most of Europe since the Middle Ages. *Salvia,* sage's botanical name, was first coined by Pliny the Elder and derives from the verb *salvere,* to "save" or "heal," in reference to this herbal plant's reputation as a medicinal colossus. There is an identifiable representation of Greek sage *(S. fruticosa)* on a fresco at Knossos on the island of Crete dating to 1400 B.C., and the use of sage's pungently scented foliage in poultices for the treatment of wounds is recorded by Theophrastus in his *Historia plantarum* of the third century B.C. and both Pliny and Dioscorides in the first century A.D.

The ancient Romans, who considered sage to be both sacred and an excellent tonic for the brain, senses, and memory, delivered it into Britain by the fourth century A.D., and, as mentioned, sage was the exalted darling of early medicants, an ancient English proverb advising, "He that would live for aye, must eat Sage in May," and an ancient French proverb avowing, "Sage helps the nerves and by its powerful might, palsy is cured and fever put to flight." *Banckes' Herbal* of 1525 says of sage, "It is a marvel that any inconvenience should grieve them that use it," and John Gerard notes, "Sage is singularly good for the head and brain, it quickeneth the senses and memory, strengtheneth the sinews, restoreth health to those that have the palsy, and taketh away shakey trembling of the members." John Evelyn sums it all up nicely in his *Acetaria* of 1699: "In short, 'tis a Plant endu'd with so many wonderful Properties, as that the aciduous use of it is said to render Men Immortal . . ."

Sage 'Icterina'

Pineapple Sage

We know now that it is sage's potent combination of volatile oils, oxygen-handling enzymes, flavonoids, and phenolic acids that give it its near-mythic antioxidant, anti-inflammatory, and antiseptic properties and, particularly, a practically unique capacity for stabilizing oxygen-related metabolism. An infusion of sage is still regarded as a valuable mitigator of feverish delirium and the "nervous excitement" that accompanies brain and nerve disorders, an excellent tonic for stomach ailments, and a first-rate antiseptic for skin complaints and abrasions.

Additionally, sages offer up a really lovely spectrum of leaf shadings, from the handsome blue-green of 'Holt's Mammoth' and 'Berggarten' to the dusky purple foliage of 'Purpurea', to the beauteous 'Icterina,' with its brilliant green-marginated-in-gold leaves, to the variegated types like 'Rainbow', with purple leaves splotched with cream and rose, and 'Tricolor', with splashes of lilac, cream, and green. As well, there's the exuberant pineapple sage *(Salvia elegans),* a subtropical variety native to Mexico, boasting bright green, defiantly un-sage-like saw-toothed leaves possessed of an amazingly strong pineapple savor and vivid scarlet blossoms.

Being mainly Mediterranean habitués, all sages will appreciate full sun and a well-drained soil and will be reliably hardy to USDA zone 8 only, although some winter mulching will increase your chances of perennial success elsewhere. John Russell's *Book of Nurture* of 1460 describes sage "frytures" as being popular at medieval banquets, so why shouldn't they be at yours? Beat a cup of flour with half a cup of beer, an egg, and a pinch of salt into a batter; dip fresh, dry sage leaves into the batter, deep-fry until puffy and browned, drain on paper towels, and serve deliciously with a honeyed vinegar dipping sauce.

Winter Savory

Savory

Satureja hortensis, S. montana

"Keep it dry by you all the year, if you love yourself and your ease, and it is a hundred pounds to a penny if you do not."

–Nicholas Culpeper, *The Complete Herbal*, 1653

The genus *Satureja,* another subset of the mint family, contains over 30 species, all basically native to the Mediterranean, with *S. hortensis,* the annual summer, or "garden," savory, and *S. montana,* the perennial winter savory, being the two types most generally grown for culinary and medicinal application. *Satureja,* bestowed upon this botanical family by Pliny the Elder, derives from *Satureia,* connoting "for the Satyrs," as these fine-scented plants were thought to belong to them. Perhaps because of this priapic association, the savories had an intriguing reputation for being able to regulate sex drive, winter savory being said to decrease it when ingested, while summer savory was thought to enhance it; so one imagines this was one good reason the summer type was preferred in most gardens.

Savory is lauded by Palladius in his *Opus agriculturae* of the fourth to fifth century A.D. and in the thirteenth century by St. Albertus Magnus, and it also rates a literary mention in William Shakespeare's *The Winter's Tale,* contestably of 1594, in the passage in which Perdita, banished to Bohemia by her father Leontes, king of Sicilia, presents blossoms to her royal visitors-in-disguise: "Here's flowers for you, hot lavender, mints, savory, marjoram . . ."

On the North American continent, the seventeenth-century English botanist John Josselyn traveled to New England and his *New-England's Rarities Discovered* of 1672 lists both summer and winter savory as two of the plants introduced there by the earliest English colonists to remind them of the gardens they had left behind. Although both savories on any continent were mainly employed as culinary herbs, like most antique food plants, they did see their share of medicinal duty, in 1629, John Parkinson recommending savory as "... effectual to expel winde ...," and the reliably vociferous Nicholas Culpeper reporting in his *Complete Herbal* of 1653, "... the Summer kind is ... both hotter and drier than the Winter kind ... It expels tough phlegm from the chest and lungs, quickens the dull spirits in the lethargy, if the juice be snuffed up the nose; dropped into the eyes it clears them of thin cold humours proceeding from the brain ..." and "...outwardly applied ... eases sciatica and palsied members."

In the end, the savories do not boast notable loads of anything in particular, with dried summer savory containing approximately 1 percent volatile oil and winter savory about 1.6 percent, both composed primarily of the phenolic monoterpene thymol, oxygen-rich carvacrol, and a smattering of triterpenic acids, amounting to some clear antioxidant activity.

Summer savory *(S. hortensis),* the culinary favorite of the two, is an annual herb, growing to about 2 feet high with oblong medium-green leaves and pretty if diminutive pink-to-blue-white flowers. Start seeds indoors 6 to 8 weeks before your frost date, then plant out 2 weeks afterwards in a sunny situation about 18 inches apart. Winter savory, on the other hand, is a dwarf perennial shrub, hardy to USDA zones 4-8, growing to about the same height, with leaves and blossoms sharing basically the same characteristics as summer savory, and may be propagated from seeds sown in spring or from cuttings or root divisions. The flavor of the savories is most often described as "thyme-y" or "peppery," so I suggest simmering green beans in salted water fragranced with a palmful of either (don't overcook!), drain, toss with a knob of butter, and top with shreds of crispy bacon if you dare.

Summer Savory

Spinach

Spinacia oleracea, Basella alba rubra, Tetragonia tetragonioides

"I'm strong to the finich, 'cause I eats me Spinach,
I'm Popeye the sailor man!"

— Popeye, circa 1933

*W*e're going to be discussing three different spinach types here, coming to us from three different species and points on the globe, the first being our familiar Popeye-brand *Spinacia oleracea,* which is believed to be of ancient Persian and Ottoman extraction, perhaps a descendant of the wild *Spinacia tetranda* that can still be found growing throughout Turkey. The first textual references to *Spinacia* came to us from Sasanian Persia (A.D. 226 to 651), and we know it was introduced into China from Nepal in A.D. 647, where it is still referred to as "the Persian green." The first Mediterranean references to our common spinach occur in the tenth century in both a medical treatise by al-Razi, the greatest Islamic physician of that period, and in the noted historian and agri-culturist Ibn Wahshiyya's *Nabataean Agriculture. Spinacia* arrived in Spain by the late twelfth century, where the great Arab agronomist Ibn al-'Awwam called it the "captain of leafy greens"; it first appeared in England and France in the four-teenth century and is mentioned in the first known English cookbook, *The Forme of Cury* (1390), where it is referred to as "spinnedge." As we know from our friend Popeye, *Spinacia oleracea* is extremely good for you, with impressive loads of vitamins A, C, and K, magnesium, manganese, iron, folate, and dietary fiber.

Indigenous to India, Africa, and other locales in Southeast Asia, Malabar spinach *(Basella alba rubra),* also known as Botany Bay Spinach, Ceylon Spinach, and Land Kelp due to its slightly seaweed-y savor, first made its way from India into Europe in 1688, when it was introduced into Holland by the Dutch governor of Malabar, and then into England in the early eighteenth century. Our third spinach, the "New Zealand" type *(Tetragonia tetragonioides),* is, as you might guess, native to New Zealand and Australia as well as Argentina, Chile, and Japan, although, oddly, it was rarely eaten in its native habitat and its first mention comes from the British explorer Captain James Cook when he had it pickled in barrels and brought onboard his ship *Endeavor* in 1770 to combat scurvy. It was the esteemed plant explorer Joseph Banks, who accompanied Cook on his voyage, who carried seeds back to Kew Gardens in England and Europe in the late eighteenth century. Malabar spinach is also a good source of vitamin A and C, a smattering of B vitamins, plus manganese, calcium, and potassium, and New Zealand Spinach is nicely high in vitamins A, K, and C and manganese.

Malabar Spinach

Spinacia oleracea is definitely a cool-weather crop and prone to bolting when temperatures climb above 75 degrees, although some of the newer hybrids are less so, which is why we include the two lesser-known species here, as they are both tropical troopers and will respond to mid-summer heat with nothing but increased vigor. There are three main types of *Spinacia oleracea:* the Savoys, with crinkly leaves, the Smooth-Leaved varieties, with broad, flat leaves, and the "Semi-Savoys," which are a hybrid of the other two. Some of the more bolt-resistant modern cultivars are 'Bloomsdale', 'Corvair', 'Melody', 'Correnta', and 'Spinner'. Malabar Spinach is an extremely vigorous viner that can grow to 30 feet or more in length, boasting succulent, white or rhubarb-red vines covered with glossy, crinkled, heart-shaped, green leaves, so do provide some stout trellising. New Zealand Spinach is also a viner but of a more crawly personality with succulent stems and small, heart-shaped leaves.

Enjoy any of these extremely good-for-you greens simply steamed then tossed with butter or olive oil and garlic.

Squash 'Sunburst'

Squash

Cucurbita pepo

"The first zucchini I ever saw, I killed with a hoe."

–John Gould, *Monstrous Depravity:*
A Jeremiad & a Lamentation About Things to Eat, 1963

The *Cucurbita pepo* family is originally native only to the southern Americas, seed remains having been found in Central America and Mexico dating to 7000 B.C., and is somewhat daunting in its immensity, including as it does pumpkins, both summer and winter squash, and ornamental gourds, all of which are pretty various in their own right. In particular, squash is a monoecious sort, so bees must do the pollinating, and because bees can carry pollen from any squash to any other, there has been considerable spontaneous hybridizing over the past 9,000 years. The difference between summer and winter squash varieties is simple: summer squash are soft-skinned and are eaten after harvest, i.e., in summer, while winter squash are notable for the thick rinds that make them storable and suitable for winter consumption.

The native tribes of North America held squash in extraordinarily high regard as one of the agricultural "three sisters" along with corn and beans, always grown together to allow the corn stalks to provide trellising for the rambling beans and squash, John Josselyn reporting in his *New-England's Rarities Discovered* of 1672, "Some of these [squash] are green, some yellow, some longish like a gourd, others round like an apple; all of them pleasant food boyled and buttered, and seasoned with spice." Squash found its way to southern Europe with the homeward-bound conquistadors,

166

the oldest known European reference dating to 1591, and were introduced into England in about 1700, where the summer types became known as "vegetable marrows," for the creaminess of their flesh, which was thought to resemble the consistency of bone marrow. However, not everyone was taken with this new food crop, the French horticulturist Olivier de Serres, who had obtained his seeds from Spain, referring to them as "Spain's revenge," and, interestingly, zucchini, although of 100 percent American stock, was actually selected and refined in Italy and reintroduced into America in the nineteenth century.

Squashes in general are not brilliant bundles of vitamins and minerals, with Vitamin C, copper, and manganese leading the fray, but they are, surprisingly, our primary edible sources of alpha-carotene and beta-carotene. Additionally, summer squash rate as one of the top three sources for the important carotenoids lutein, zeaxanthin, and beta-cryptoxanthin.

As discussed, there are a nearly infinite number of squash cultivars to consider for culture, so the best I can do again here is name some favorites we grow on the farm. In the summer squash category, we always grow a diminutive round zucchini like 'Ronde de Nice' or 'Eight Ball', as these squash never grow to dog size, looking like the blissful love child of a zucchini and a tennis ball; we also grow the pretty pattypan types like the bright yellow 'Sunburst', the deep green 'Starship', and the heirloom 'Benning's Green Tint'. In terms of winter varieties, our familiar Acorns, Butternuts, and Hubbards are all excellent choices, but we also look towards lesser-known but very tasty varieties like the white-and-green-striated 'Delicata', the delicious 'Sweet Dumpling', and the fascinating-fleshed 'Spaghetti' squash.

In terms of culture, all squash like the soil and weather well warmed up. Therefore, start any in 4-inch pots about a month before last frost, then plant out in well-fertilized hills, 3 plants to a hill, hills 4 feet apart, when soil temperature is above 60 degrees. Thin to the strongest two plants per hill.

For summer squash varieties, why not employ them in a classic ratatouille with tomatoes, peppers, and onions, and for the winter types, who can resist an acorn squash baked with its cavity awash with maple syrup and butter?

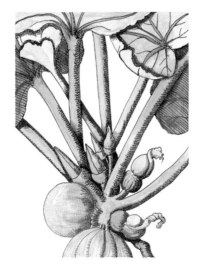

Squash 'Ronde de Nice'

Strawberry

Fragaria ananassa

*"Doubtless God could have made a better berry,
but doubtless God never did."*

—Dr. William Butler (1536–1617)

The wild strawberry is anciently native to every continent save Africa, Australia, and New Zealand, and its first rather ominous literary mention seems to take place in Italy in Virgil's *Third Ecologue* of about 40 B.C., in which the shepherd Damoetas is warned: "Ye boys that gather flowers and strawberries, Lo, hid within the grass an adder lies." Ovid gives the strawberry a merrier nod in his description of the Golden Age from his epic *Metamorphoses*, completed in A.D. 8: "The teeming Earth, yet guiltless of the plough, And unprovok'd, did fruitful stores allow: Content with food, which Nature freely bred, On wildings and on strawberries they fed . . ."

The tiny wood strawberry *(Fragaria vesca)* was brought into cultivation in France in the fourteenth century, and by 1368, the French King Charles V was ordering 1,200 strawberry plants to be planted in the gardens of the Louvre. By the mid-seventeenth century, Roger Williams, founder of Rhode Island, was marveling at New England's amazing abundance of wild strawberries, observing, "I have many times seen as many as would fill a good ship," and America's first great botanist, William Bartram, wrote in 1773, during his exploration of the American South, of strawberry fields so

Strawberry 'Tristar'

Strawberry 'Earliglow'

vast and plentiful that they dyed the legs of his horses as they rode through. It is believed to be Thomas Hariot, Sir Walter Raleigh's scientific adviser, who first relayed the native American strawberry *(Fragaria virginiana)* to England in 1585, and there is clear evidence that the French spy Amedée François Frézier delivered the first 'Chili' strawberry *(Fragaria chiloensis)* into France from Chile in 1714. In 1759, Philip Miller, director of the Chelsea Physics Garden in London, describes a strawberry obtained from George Clifford, director of the Netherlands East India Company, and most taxonomists now identify the 'Miller' strawberry as the first cultivated offspring of the Virginia strawberry and the 'Chili.' Called "Pineapple" or "Pine" strawberries *(Fragaria ananassa),* as their scent was thought to resemble that of the pineapple (thus *ananassa),* these late-eighteenth-century cultivars are the antecedents of all modern cultured varieties.

The ancient Romans believed wild strawberries could cure everything from bouts of fainting, inflammations, fevers, and halitosis, to all diseases of the blood, liver, and spleen, and modern science has confirmed that strawberries are a treasure trove of nutrition, containing both ellagic acid, which is powerfully antioxidant, and flavonoids, and a single cup will deliver 140 percent of your daily dose of vitamin C.

There are two basic subsets of the modern strawberry, their division based on fruiting and flowering: the "June-bearing" types, requiring short days, cool temperatures, and bearing fruit only in spring, and the "ever-bearing" varieties, which, as the name would suggest, yield fruit throughout the growing season. Some of the most popular June-bearing types are 'Earliglow', 'Honeoye', 'Sparkle', 'Clancy', and 'Surecrop', and, in the ever-bearing category, 'Tristar', 'Quinault', 'Tribute', 'Ozark Beauty', and 'Eversweet' head the list; but, as in other cases we have explored, it will be wise to quiz your local USDA Extension or nursery for the best cultivars for your zone and climate.

Culturally, strawberries are a snap: plant about a foot apart in sandy to loamy soil with good drainage, pinching off flowers in the first season to encourage runners. Plants may then fruit for two or three seasons, then will need renovation in the fourth when fruit quality and yield start to wane. For these scrumptious and healthful berries, the early British horticulturist Thomas Hyll informs us in his *Gardener's Labyrinth* of 1593 that they were "much eaten at all men's tables in the sommer time with wine and sugar," which sounds like a heavenly idea.

Tarragon

Artemisia dracunculus, Tagetes lucida

"Ruellius and such others have reported many strange tales hereof . . . saying that the seed of flax put into a Raddish root or sea Onion, and so set, doth bring forth this herbe Tarragon."

–John Gerard, *The Herball*, 1636

*A*lthough most gastronomes will insist there is only one true tarragon, the French sort *(Artemisia dracunculus)*, I am determined to also champion its far more vigorous cousin Mexican Tarragon *(Tagetes lucida)* here. I have purposefully chosen to eschew the third type, Russian tarragon *(A. dracunculoides L.)*, as it is decidedly culinarily inferior to the other two. Whatever the seventeenth-century French botanist Johannes Ruellius believed, French tarragon is not the mixed-marriage offspring of flax and radish but an Artemisia constituent native to Mongolia and Siberia, while *Tagetes lucida* is native to Mexico and Central America alone.

French tarragon is thought to have been introduced into Italy from the Black Sea somewhere around the tenth century A.D. and was carried into England about 1548, during the sadly short reign of the boy-king Edward VII. Interestingly, while most herbs have a long history of medicinal employment, tarragon is oddly lacking in much more than culinary application, John Gerard also reporting in his *Herball* of 1636, "Tarragon is not to be eaten alone in sallades, but joyned with other herbs, as Lettuce, Purslain, and such like, that it may also temper the coldnesse of them . . . neither do we know what other use this herbe hath." However, Nicholas Culpeper, in his *Complete Herball* of 1653, allows that "the leaves . . . are heating and drying, and good for those who have the flux, or any preternatural discharge," with John Evelyn endorsing tarragon in his *Acetaria* of 1699 as " . . . highly cordial and friend to the head, heart and liver."

Additionally, we know that Mexican tarragon was employed by the Aztecs for a variety of ailments, from the common cold and colic to malaria and fever, and in an interesting duality of cultures, the ancient Greeks used French tarragon as a treatment for toothache, while Mexican tarragon was reportedly employed by the Aztecs in a

170

powder blown into the faces of victims of human sacrifice to sedate them before the dirty deed, modern medicine affirming that both types get their pain-killing properties from the natural anesthetic eugenol.

French tarragon is also an excellent source of vitamins C, A, and B6, magnesium, iron, zinc, and calcium, and extracts of Mexican tarragon have been found to possess excellent antimicrobial, antibacterial, and antioxidant properties.

As mentioned, culinary royalty are insistent that there is no substitute for French tarragon's subtle, sweet, licorice-like savor; however, French tarragon is not the most trouble-free herb we have ever cultured on the farm, which is why I am insistent on including the Mexican variety as being both easier and heartier in terms of culture and, if not so sweetly subtle as the French sort, also possessing immense culinary appeal. Interestingly, I can find no evidence of named cultivars of these cousins: just "French" and "Mexican." Additionally, while you may start the Mexican type from seed, French tarragon must be propagated by root or stem division, so you will start with a plant in that case. Both species will succeed best in a hot, dry situation and both will reward you with tasty leaves and sunny yellow flowers in late summer.

Because tarragon loses its flavor rapidly when dried, fresh is always best. Pickling was a popular way to keep it, so surely every kitchen deserves a big bottle of home-made tarragon vinegar: stuff a half dozen sprigs of either variety into a tall bottle, fill with white or cider vinegar, cork, and steep on a sunny windowsill for several weeks.

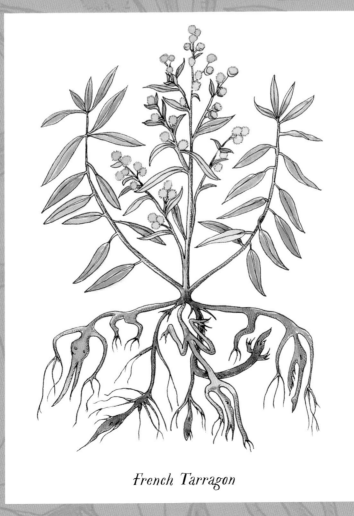

French Tarragon

Thyme

Thymus spp.

"Thestilis for mowers tyr'd with parching heate,
Garlicke, wilde Time, strong smelling herbes doth beate."
—Virgil, *Eclogues,* 44–38 B.C.

*T*hyme is a genus of about 350 aromatic plants in the sprawling *Lamiaceae* (mint) family. Native to Europe, North Africa, and Asia, its earliest recorded mention occurs in Sumeria in 3000 B.C., where it was noted, as in many subsequent cultures, including our own, as a powerful antiseptic. The Egyptians utilized thyme in their mummification processes, and, in close parallel employment, the ancient Greeks placed it in the coffins of the dead, assuring their passage into the afterlife, and made use of it for purifying sacrifices to make them acceptable to the gods, as well as a fumigant against illness and disease and as a chief ingredient in ritual altar fires.

Thyme is thought to originate in the Greek *thumus,* either signifying "smoke" (by way of the Latin *fumos*), in reference to this herb's antique role as fumigant and sacrificial incense, or "courage," as thyme was thought to engender it with its "cordial qualities" (W. T. Fernie, *Herbal Simples,* 1914). Tradition also holds that thyme was a component of what has come to be known as "Our Lady's Bedstraw," which lined the Savior's cradle on that long-ago Christmas Eve.

The ancient Romans, much like the Greeks and Egyptians, used thyme to purify their rooms, and soldiers were known to bathe in thyme-scented water before going into battle to engender courage, ultimately spreading it throughout Europe with their conquests. By the Middle Ages, Lancastrian ladies in England were habitually bestowing tokens of thyme on their errant knights to render them courageous. In 1629, John Parkinson claims it useful as a "remedy for shortness of breath . . . kills worms in the belly . . . helps the sciatica and dullness of sight . . ." and ". . . comforts the stomach much and expels wind . . . ," while in 1636, John Gerard recommends thyme for the apparently always anciently

Lemon Thyme 'Silver Queen'

problematic "bitings of any venomous beast." We now know the volatile oil thymol is the key constituent here, and recent studies have confirmed that it is fiercely anti-oxidant and is capable of not only increasing the amount of DHA (docosahexaenoic acid), a notably potent omega-3 fatty acid, in brain, kidney, and heart cell membranes, but is also impressively antimicrobial against a battery of bacteria and fungi.

As noted, there are many comely varieties of thyme, ranging from that culinary champ the green-leaved common garden thyme *(T. vulgaris)* to the carpet-like types (woolly thyme, *T. pseudolanuginosus*) to varieties scented of caraway *(T. herba-barona),* orange *(T. vulgaris* var. *odoratissimus),* lime *(T. citriodorus),* or lemon, like the lovely variegated 'Silver Queen' (*T. citriodorus* 'Silver Queen'), and others with golden leaves (*T. vulgaris* 'Aureus') or colorful marginations *(T. argenteus).*

We always plant five or six types on the farm, including between pavers in stone pathways and in the rock garden border around our pool, for I am in perfect agreement with Sir Francis Bacon, who, as Dr. Fernie relates, ". . . recommends to set whole alleys of Thyme for the pleasure of the perfume when treading on the plant." All thymes will reward you with that signature camphor-y/pine-y scent and whorls of tiny white-to-pink-to-purple blossoms, all will prefer a warm, sunny situation and well-drained soil, most are perennially hardy to USDA zone 5, and all will appreciate a good mulching of crowns in winter.

In the kitchen, rub minced garlic and some thyme over any roast, use it to fragrance a classic Italian sauce, or throw a healthful handful into an assortment of steamed and buttered fresh vegetables, and let your imagination guide you to further gastronomic heights.

173

Tomato 'Elberta Peach'   *Tomato 'Tiger Tom'*   *Tomato 'Sweet Million'*

Tomato

Solanum lycopersicon esculentum

*When the tomato, or "Moors Apple" (pomei di moro), was
introduced to France, the always up for fun French
mistook the name to be "pomo d'amour," and so the designation
of the tomato as "love apple" was born.*

*I*n the annals of vegetable history, the tomato must certainly claim the crown as the edible plant with the most dramatic gastronomic turnaround, for although it was viciously maligned by a host of cultures, including our own, well into the nineteenth century, the tomato now stands as the single most popular vegetable in current Western culture.

It originated spontaneously in the coastal highlands of western South America and small, scruffy wild tomatoes can still be found growing in the seaside mountains of Peru, Chile, and Ecuador. The wild tomato was a simple two-celled creature until a friendly genetic mutation occurred, resulting in the large, lobed, multi-celled fruit with which we are now so familiar. Tomatoes were delivered to the European continent by the homeward-bound Spanish conquistadors in the fifteenth century, but as members of the always-suspect Solanum or nightshade family, they were promptly given the designation of "wolf's peach," or Lycopersicon, the name given to an unknown and perhaps mythical fruit by the second century A.D. Greek physician Galen, as night-shades were legendarily linked to werewolves. The tomato-bashing continued in 1544, when the Italian herbalist Pietro Andrae Matthioli referred to the new import as *mala aurea,* or "bad golden thing," and the English herbalist John Gerard, who planted them in the College of Physicians gardens in Holborne in 1590, concluded that "the whole plant" was possessed "of ranke and stinking savour." Karl Linnaeus managed to add the *esculentum,* meaning "edible," in the eighteenth century, although this was an issue still clearly up for debate.

North America, which bizarrely only welcomed the tomato when it was introduced from Europe in the eighteenth century, had much the same reaction, Joseph T. Buckingham, early-nineteenth-century editor of the *Boston Courier,* calling the tomato "the mere fungus of an offensive plant, which one cannot touch without an immediate application of soap and water . . . ," and even as late as 1836, S. D. Wilcox, editor of the *Florida Agriculturist,* pronounced his first tomato "an arrant humbug" that "deserved forthwith to be consigned to the tomb of all the Capulets." Of course, we now know that America's favorite edible plant to know and grow is swooningly delicious at its best as well as an excellent source of vitamins A and C, lycopene, magnesium, and iron.

Tomato 'German Red Strawberry'

Tomato 'Green Zebra'

Tomato 'Purple Calabash'

Tomatoes come in a huge variety of sizes, shapes, and colorations, ranging from currant-sized to 2-pound mammoths, round to "ox-hearted" to totally misshapen, black, dark purple, and red to orange, yellow, green, and white, ribbed or lobed or both, so I will again here serve you up some of our favorites on the farm. Notable among these are the brawny, bi-colored beefsteak 'Hillbilly', the super sweet cherries 'SunGold' and 'Sweet Million', that Moby Dick of tomatoes 'Great White', the prettily striated types 'Green Zebra' and 'Tiger Tom', the lycopene-rich Russian "blacks" like 'Black From Tula', and 'Black Krim', and the whole heirloom 'Brandywine' family. Tomatoes are a fairly long-season idea, so start in the greenhouse in 4-inch pots 4 to 6 weeks before last frost, then plant deeply (right up to their necks to promote a good root system) in a well-composted, sunny spot when soil temperature is above 60 degrees, and harvest in about 80 to 90 days from transplant.

Why not coarse-chop a few of any variety and toss with chopped fresh mint, crumbled blue cheese, and a lemony vinaigrette for a nice variation on a classic Caprese salad?

21 20 19 18 17   5 4 3 2

Text © 2017 Jack Staub
Illustrations © 2017 Ellen Sheppard Buchert

Published by
Gibbs Smith
P.O. Box 667
Layton, Utah 84041

1.800.835.4993 orders
www.gibbs-smith.com

Designed by Sky Hatter

Printed and bound in Hong Kong

Gibbs Smith books are printed on either recycled, 100% post-consumer waste, FSC-certified
papers or on paper produced from sustainable PEFC-certified forest/controlled wood source.
Learn more at www.pefc.org.

Library of Congress Cataloging-in-Publication Data
Names: Staub, Jack, 1951- author.
Title: The illustrated book of edible plants / Jack Staub ; illustrations
by Ellen Buchert.
Description: First edition. | Layton, Utah : Gibbs Smith, 2017.
Identifiers: LCCN 2016032640 | ISBN 9781423646747 (jacketless hardcover)
Subjects: LCSH: Plants, Edible. | Food crops.
Classification: LCC QK98.5.A1 S73 2017 | DDC 581.6/32--dc23
LC record available at https://lccn.loc.gov/2016032640
ISBN: 9781423646747